TEMPTATIONS

WHEN AND WHY THEY COME

SILVANUS OLUOCH

Great Ministries Publishers

TEMPTATIONS

WHEN AND WHY THEY COME

Great Ministries Publishers

Temptations

ISBN: 9966-9991-0-8

Scripture quotations unless otherwise indicated, are from the
Authorized King James Version
The ones marked Living Bible are from the Living Bible
©Tyndale House Publishers 1971

The ones marked Amplified Bible are from the Amplified
Bible © Zondervan Publishing House 1965. Used by
permission.

Permission will be given to anyone requesting the use of any
part of this book for the purpose of gospel propagation and
furtherance of truth.

Published by Great Ministries Publishers
The Literature Division of Great Ministries
P.O. Box 69163, 00610
Nairobi, Kenya.

*No temptation has you in its power but such as is common to human nature; and God is faithful and will not allow you to be tempted beyond your strength. But, **when the temptation comes**, He will also provide the way of escape; so that you may be able to bear it.*
1Corinthians 10:13

To Joab Odhiambo Adipo who knows how far grace has
brought us

Contents

Chapter One
Simple Meaning of Temptation 13

Chapter Two
General Facts about Temptations 21

Chapter Three
Where Do Temptations Come From? 41

Chapter Four
Keen Look at Jesus' Temptations 57

Chapter Five
How to Face Temptations 69

Chapter Six
Purpose of Temptations 81

Chapter Seven
Deliverance in Temptations 87

Chapter Eight
The General Means of Deliverance in Temptations 91

Chapter Nine
Summary of Facts about Temptations 105

Last Word 109

INTRODUCTION

It is reported that Martin Luther almost gave up on his stay when he first entered the Monastery. He had presumed he would be safe from the devil and all his temptations when he went into that place. However, he found himself vexed with temptations even right inside the Monastery. That is the frame of mind some of us have; sometimes we try escaping from temptations by going into places we presume to be secure and safe from them like Churches, Convents, and such like places. Nevertheless, there is no safe shelter from temptations. Temptations are universal life phenomena that can face anyone anywhere anytime. That means, no one can escape temptations as long as they are alive.

My purpose in this writing is to present the reader with some general healthy information on temptations, and to show them basic dynamics involved in any temptation set-up. I will also be endeavoring to help the reader understand the great resources God has for His children undergoing temptations. With that understanding it would then be unnecessary for anyone to fear temptations.

I will also be pointing out that "blame shifting", where most people shift blame to the devil for their every temptation is a cop out. It has been well portrayed, in the recent past, by the American comedian Flip Wilson in his household line *"the devil made me do it"*. Sadly, some Christians are hooked on to that same line and keep blaming the devil in almost every bad situation in their lives. Poignantly, some Christian ministries, especially the so-called spiritual warfare movements are built on this premise. They see the devil almost in everything.

Nevertheless, the truth is that the natural person has been conditioned to always blame someone else when caught on the wrong side of life. This is observable as early as Eden when Adam blamed God for having given him the wife, whom he claimed led him into the disobedience. Further in the Bible we come across Aaron, who blamed the Israelites for their being prone to sin what he claimed led him to make them a golden calf! (Exodus 32:22). Even Saul the first King of Israel when caught in disobedience to God, blamed his fighters for having spared the best and fattest rams from Amalek. (1Samuel 15:15).

But all those were just excuses these people brought forth trying to save face, yet deep within they knew they were wrong. Though people continue blame shifting even today, it is important to realize that it is not the devil who makes people do bad things in all cases. People themselves when they yield to or indulge their selfish desires end up with some of those unfortunate situations.

I have written on the general principles of this phenomenon without being technical, and I trust I have addressed most of the common hang-ups people usually have on temptations.

Silvanus

CHAPTER ONE

SIMPLE MEANING OF TEMPTATION

Temptation can simply be defined as a solicitation to do or involve in an unaccepted activity. It involves getting attracted to do things you are not supposed to. In a religious sense it is solicitation to evil or unethical acts. It is simply the disguised allurement to do wrong. The desire to sacrifice the future on the altar of the present. That is; what could be of great importance in the future is squandered for its own sake in the present. This is sometimes called, having your cake and eating it. It begins with *doubting* God, then *lusting* after the very things He forbids. Then we move on to acting, and ending up *disobeying* God in actually moving ahead to do that which we know he prohibits.

It is a natural phenomenon that confronts people with choice-making; either positively or negatively. On the positive side it is simply a test, while on the negative it is a lure. Whenever one chooses negatively they fail the temptation. In Christian lingo that is called falling into sin. But temptation in itself is not sin, neither is it something bad to be avoided at any cost. Yielding to it is what is wrong.

Generally, some people fear being tempted because they do not want to fail. They do not know how it may turn out; presumably they believe that if they are never tempted they will be okay. This is because they only associate temptation with evil and failure. That is the reason they try, as much as they can to live their lives quietly without the intrusion of this thing called temptation. However, with proper understanding this should not be the case.

EVEN JESUS WAS TEMPTED

The Bible informs us that the Holy Spirit led Jesus into the wilderness to be tempted, and from that statement we understand that temptation is not an evil experience. If it were, the Holy Spirit would not have led Jesus into it. Temptation, as such, is good for us; it is a flip side of God's testing. It serves a great purpose in God's plans for us, if we understand it thus. It is simply a test; testing our character, personality and moral standing and our allegiance to whatever standards we subscribe to. More so, to the Christians it tests our commitment to God and His word. This is the reason Jesus also had to take that test, since He had taken upon Himself a creaturely nature of the humans.

NOT OCCASIONED BY GOD

Even so, it is not God who brings temptations to us. He allows them to come as life situations and circumstances that arrive, either as tests or temptations dependent on where our allegiances are strong. When our allegiances are strong on God's side such phenomenon to us becomes tests, while they are allurement when our allegiances are strong on the opposite side. They come through our normal life circumstances for the purposes of testing and proving us. So much so because to be perfected or matured up, every intelligible moral being must be subjected to some sort of tests. And this is done through circumstances that generate opportunities for choice making, as the means of propelling us forward into higher levels of involvement with God.

Therefore, on the side of God such opportunities for choice making are tests while on the human and the enemy's side they are temptations.

They do not come to wreck us, for God is not in the business of wrecking people. But He is rather in the business of developing and establishing us for His Kingdom reign. This preparation He does through the various agencies and processes some involving trials. This is the reason it has been said that trials help us become the people of God's full intentions. In them our innocence is broken on the platform of options for choice making as we break free from merely following instincts. At it we are rather made to distinguish between the alternatives of good and evil.

It is important, therefore, to understand that it is not God who tempts people. The Bible says:

> *Let no man say when he is tempted, I am tempted of God. For God cannot be tempted with evil, Neither tempteth, He any man: But every man is tempted, when he is drawn away of his own lust, and enticed,* **James 1:13-14**.

It is inconceivable to imagine that God would tempt anyone in the sense of luring them to evil; He has got no evil intentions and cannot lure anyone into evil. His moral nature and holiness cannot let that happen. It is contrary to everything He is. Thus the tests or trials that come from Him are for the splendid purpose rather than being an avenue to evil.

Nevertheless, it has been observed that whatever God intends for testing and proving us, the devil on the other hand perverts to use for tempting us instead. And he does that with a view to defeating and destroying us. His underlying desire is to hinder and break our fellowship with God and our remaining in His purposes. That is how it is in the whole of life; God's good intentions the devil perverts to hurt people. The chief example here is sex, a wonderful human expressive enjoyment. But see what the devil has done with it. Look at families and life itself. The devil seems to be perverting everything. Good and perfect gifts are turning into bad things that generate incongruous painful experiences.

In the Bible, especially beginning from Genesis we see this example. We are introduced to God planting the Garden of Eden and its various trees in Genesis 2. Even the famous tree of knowledge of good and evil was planted there by God not by Satan. This tells us that that tree was good as all things God created were. This then implies that that tree must have had a purpose in God's greater overall plan. Insightfully, we know that He intended it to be an emblem through which the human was to be tested for obedience as he developed in his relationship with God. Like has been stated, obedience is not automatic; it is learned and proven through tests and trials to where trust is the outcome. It cannot be ascertained otherwise, except through the means of the trials and temptations. The Bible intimates that even Jesus learned obedience through the things He underwent. Everyone has to undergo something in order to learn something.

We glean from the beginning that God had pronounced the finished work of creating the humans as very good. Thus, we gather that the humans were good, but untested. That means they were good as created, but stood untested. No wonder, God had incorporated a scheme in His divine plans that He was going to use to test and bring out, or manifest that goodness in mankind. Such a test was intended to move the humans from *positional goodness* to practical or real-life goodness involving character formation through growth processes. He was then put in the garden environment to give him a platform and the opportunity to act out his true nature of goodness. That is where the Tree of the Knowledge of good and evil comes into play. It was the testing instrument intended to bring the best out of man's personality. It was to show his level of development and dependence on His God.

Clearly, it could also reveal the underdeveloped areas of his being within God's intentions for him then. Character quality and capacity were already ingrained in Adam at creation, yet deeply buried in him. It was going to take the process of growth and development, especially under pressures of trials and testing to finally manifest those qualities. But the tragedy here was that Adam personally was seemingly ignorant of God's objective for him, and for that tree he was commanded not to eat from. He let go his allegiance to God in an attempt to try making his own discoveries in life by eating from the tree he was forbidden. As a result he unceremoniously cut himself off from the real life.

But the testing was not meant to crash or wreck him. Yet we see that the devil took advantage of it and used it for man's downfall. The devil perverted God's testing emblem into a temptation tool. This bespeaks that in every temptation there is always an element of testing that God intends for our good, if only we can discern it. But on the other side there is the devil waiting to pervert the same to our detriment.

The same is true when we move over into the New Testament, especially within the temptations of Jesus in the wilderness. His going out there after the wonderful River Jordan experience was all about the testing of His person and character in regards to His allegiance to God. God had publicly declared Him the Son of His pleasure and love. As Jesus was being baptized the heavens opened up and the Holy Spirit like a dove was seen descending upon Him. Then the

Father's voice was heard declaring Jesus as His beloved Son in whom He is well pleased. Jesus is the Son of God's supreme love; the beloved Son. Yet, how was that going to play out in His personal daily life away from Jordan? Was He going to maintain being the son of God's pleasure?

That was what the wilderness test was to reveal; His dependency on God or on Himself. When He took on the human nature; Jesus embraced dependence and limitability, which are some of the same qualities Adam was created with. That means humans by nature even before the fall, were created dependent and limited. Therefore, like everyone else Jesus was being thrust into the practicality of experiencing human life. A life that requires total dependency on God.

He could depend on God, since He understood His limitations of the human nature; or He could device His own ways of existence as Adam had tried. Then when He got into His tests, as usual the enemy appeared and turned the tests into temptations. All that with a view to defeating God's purpose for Him. There and then we see the devil taking what God meant for good and turning it into something negative; something to use to destroy others. He came along and found Jesus in the wilderness engaged in fasting and involvement with His Father. The devil then begun to draw His attention away to other factors. He began telling Jesus how hungry He must have been since He had not eaten in a long time. But he was unaware of what must have transpired between the Father and His Son for the thirty some days that Jesus had engaged heaven.

Of course, much had transpired between the Father and the Son before the devil came to the scene. As a by the way, the devil came quite late after Jesus had spent forty days and nights involving with heaven. No wonder, Jesus finally just took authority over him and he had to flee.

From God's standpoint what we see or consider as temptation is simply a test or trial for our betterment. If we see it that way then we can embrace and experience it as an opportunity for our development in grace. That is one of the reasons why God does not insulate us from temptations as we often desire. It would be better if every time we see the word temptation that we look at it from God's point of view. That will reveal it as a test meant for our good.

Austin T Sparks, a preacher of the past century commenting on this said that the Lord neither puts us in glass houses to grow us . . . nor does He protect us from the storms and adversities. Rather He exposes us to bitter winds (of life) and scotching suns of adversity and trial. With all that, He is working in us that which is according to His own nature – eternity, the enduring . . . that which will not be easily or hardly carried away. He is putting substance into us; that steadfast enduring faithfulness so we can endure throughout all ages. It is His way of deepening us and putting caliber into us.

CHAPTER TWO

GENERAL FACTS ABOUT TEMPTATIONS

Temptations involve:
- ❖ selfish choice making
- ❖ accepting a false image
- ❖ enticement as part of it
- ❖ make-believe aspect to it

TEMPTATION DRAWS ON OUR SELFISHNESS

We live either in the kingdom of light or the one of darkness and the choices we make, fall in either of these. Christians are children of the kingdom of light, and when they choose and execute things of the kingdom of darkness; they betray their Kingdom. This means the Christians are not supposed to yield to suggestions either *internal* or *external*, which make them choose the kingdom of darkness. Note that I have used the terms external and *internal* suggestions, because it is not always the external suggestions what bring us temptations. But more so, the internal influences; right from the depth of our beings!

One preacher put it that if we think it is always the external influences what lead to temptation then we are wrong. He asked an astounding question about who tempted the **devil** to rebel against God in the first place, if temptation is always a response to external stimuli. And the natural answer is that no one tempted the devil; there was no external influence on Lucifer then. His temptation was all from within him. That is where every temptation springs from; within the intelligent being.

This means even in our cases temptation may seem to be coming from outside, yet it is drawn by something in us. That means the external attraction is usually occasioned by something within you. It means you cannot be tempted with what does not appeal to you. That appeal springs from within you and then finds a corresponding attraction externally. It may be temptation to worry, lust, tell lies, cheat, steal, fear, bribe and fight or be unfair and so forth. But they all ride on and find expressions through our fallen nature within our choice options.

Thus, there was within Satan a created quality of choice he could use, just like all of us. He had to make a choice based on the fact that he was an intelligent being. Then as life progressed, he came to the realization that he was free to exercise his choice-making anyhow. After this, it is probable he began to toy with an idea though remote then, about giving vent to his personal desires other than that for which he was created. We understand that he was created with much beauty and probably made to lead in the worship of God. The Bible says in Ezekiel that:

> *The workmanship of thy tabrets and of thy pipes was in thee;*
> *in the day that thou wast created they were prepared.*
> **Ezekiel 28:13**

Here we see that Satan's artistic and musical abilities were inherent in him from creation. It is further intimated that he was set upon the mountain of God. It looks like from there, he was to lead the worship of God Almighty, and that must have gone on for countless ages in eternity past. But then this subtle little thing within him; the desire to **divert the worship of God to himself,** and to be like God could not leave him. He toyed with it long enough until it conceived and like James says:

"Then when lust hath conceived, it bringeth forth sin . . ."
James 1:15.

His lust for God's glory and authority birthed sin. This seemingly portrays that sin did not exist prior to this, but was birthed from within him as a principle. However, he did not create it; it was a subsequent effect. That means sin was not created, but came into existence as a result of a selfish and negative choice of a created intelligent being. When the devil chose to indulge his own egoistic desires to acquire God's glory; the reaction to his act in the serene atmosphere of God's glorious life resulted into a negative force called sin. It is a known fact that sin does not exist independently on its own. It is simply the expression of a selfish will within an intelligent created being. It is a turning away from God to live or act independent of Him, rejecting His design and requirements.

Thus, sin arises from within those who have departed from the living God. All known created intelligent beings are endowed with the ability to choose and whenever they choose to (depart from) be independent of God; sin rears its ugly head. And that is what Lucifer did. The reaction within his life to his rebellion against God turned into a real negative and viral condition called sin.

Like I have stated in my book *Holy Angels;* that could have been the point in existence when he then declared his famous five "I wills" as found in Isaiah 14:12-14.

- I *will* ascend into heaven
- I *will* exalt my throne above the stars of God
- I *will* also sit on the mount of the congregation
- I *will* ascend above the heights of the clouds
- I *will* be like the most High

The word "**I**" stood out clearly in his statements and true enough to his desires, he went ahead and tried to be like the Most High God. However, that was the most unfortunate step he undertook; choosing **self** in disregard to God and it brought a total change into the created existence. He did not care much about God then, but was only concerned about his own supremacy. Unfortunately, that move plunged the whole created order into disarray. Oh, how tragic! But it was and so sin entered into the scene. But you can see that there was no external influence on him to do what he did. It was all from within him; his desires and presumptions. James in his letters points out this very clearly when he says:

*"But every man is tempted when he is drawn away of **his own lust** and enticed."* **James 1:14**.

James says nothing at all about the external influences but the preoccupation with oneself – **drawn away by his own lust and is enticed.** This is true because it is possible in all ways and is within the human heart to sin even with the *devil a thousand miles away!* Though not accepted by many people, mankind is his greatest and number one enemy; 'everyone is his own enemy', said St. Bernard. And Prophet Jeremiah confirms this when he asserts that:

"The (human) heart is deceitful above all things and desperately wicked..." **Jeremiah 17:9**. Word in bracket is mine.

We should discard the common notion that whenever there is sin or temptation; or even problems then it is because of the devil. We must realize that **self;** the old sinful nature is a potential source of temptations in itself even without the devil. In fact, it is a big hindrance to the smooth development of our inner lives. Though people always attribute what generally comes from the dispositions and impressions of their fallen natures to the devil; that is merely giving him unnecessary credits. That in itself is akin to worshipping him.

It is not necessarily because of the devil that humans have problems, or engage in the weird things they do. It is simply because of who they are; fallen beings who inherited a broken nature from Adam. Thus, there is need to be balanced in our outlooks and stop blaming the devil for everything.

Someone painted a humorous picture about this when he said that one morning Mr. Devil sat by a neighborhood roadside crying. And a fellow from that neighborhood saw him and inquired what was wrong. He asked Mr. Devil the reason he was crying that early in the morning. To which Mr. Devil answered that he was weighted down by the human accusations. He was tired of being accused and blamed for all the wrong things in humans' lives. He explained that some of the human situations he knew nothing about; yet are all blamed on him! He conveyed that people always accuse and blame him for all sorts of things they do from their own selfishness.

They blame it all on him, claiming he made them do it. Yet they are usually drawn to such situations (the temptations) by their own inclinations and desires. The devil never drags anyone to any temptation situations; people take themselves to those situations, drawn or pulled to by their own lusts. It is only after they have arrived there that he begins his work in temptations, which is basically to **entice them.** That is, he seduces them as to the goodness or the profitability of the ideas they are already toying with. Basically this means the *devil* without, only finds his power (strength) from the *evil* within us. If there is nothing in you that attracts the devil he will not tempt you. That something is us, which appeals to the devil is what Paul called "sin that dwelleth in us".

Even in the Garden of Eden Eve was not dragged to the tree of the knowledge of good and evil by anyone, but by her lust. This is what James' statement means:

"But every man is tempted when he is drawn away of **his own lust** and enticed." **James 1:14.**

As she was walking in the garden, something (lust or curiosity) within her drew her to that tree. She then stood there long enough looking at it and then the devil took that opportunity to entice her. The devil began convincing her with untrue *facts* about the goodness of that particular tree. This all happened because she was there.

FOCUSING ON THE DEVIL UNHEALTHY

As we have observed, focusing on the devil is unhealthy for spiritual and even physical wellbeing. Someone has claimed that doing so is a form of devil worship. This was depicted by the story of two friends who got into a heated argument, because one had called the other a devil worshipper. But then a sagacious man who overheard them, and wanted to stall their argument explained what it really meant to worship the devil. It is to give the devil unnecessary credits, and or to ascribe to him powers he doesn't have. According to him such is done when people; unawares, have strong affinity to the devil rather than God.

He went on to explain to them that there are those who have wrong concepts of the devil and hence, claim falsely about him. They presume that the devil hears every word they utter, or that the devil stands around calculating to do them evil all the time. They even believe that he is always scheming to thwart God's purposes for them. Thus, they are fascinated with the devil unawares. They constantly talk about him, unnecessarily giving him credits he doesn't deserve. They end up paying him homage unawares.

For instance, they take it upon themselves, in their misconceptions to keep "binding" him. They term that commanding and rebuking the devil. But there is no warrant for such an act in the Bible. It is a misconception drawn from the book of Matthew taking about "whatever the disciples were to bind or loose on earth would have a corresponding action in heaven". They take it out of context and mostly apply it to binding the devil, which even none of the apostle ever did.

However, this devil they bind keeps breaking loose and bounces right back into their next meeting or gathering. So they have to keep binding him (whatever that is) every time. Occasionally, they presume to have bound him forever, but come next meeting and the war rages on. They sense him and have to bind him again and again, or some of his minions. Their sensitivity is to the devil and their lives are a constant state of devil-consciousness.

Thus, anytime they do not get an immediate answer to their prayers; they accuse the devil for hindering it. And when things don't seem to work for them or go contrary to their plans; they are sure it is the devil interfering. They see devils and demons in everything. When setbacks come, say a car accident then they conclude it is the devil fighting them. It is just them and the devil, with God in the periphery like a fetish they try to use to defeat the devil.

Their prayers are punctuated with "this devil and that devil we bind you . . . or . . . we bind you spirit of this and that." Their faith seems to be more on the devil or demons than in God or Jesus. In their presumptions, they keep on being fascinated with the devil, and attribute so much powers and mischief to him unnecessarily. All they do has nothing to do with real praying to God or Jesus. It has nothing to do with God's sovereignty. It is simply a form of devil worship. This unexpected explanation surprised and was insightful to both men!

Generally, temptation can be likened to being at crossroads knowing which way to go, yet a suggestion leaning towards the wrong road pops up urging us to choose it. Immediately, a tag of war begins within us because temptation excites our curiosity to search out and experience the alternative. The curiosity then combines with self-interests in us and urgent desire to explore and find out what lies on the other side. It vehemently takes center stage in our thoughts. That is, we know what is right in a particular situations, yet the desire within us to find out about the unknown becomes resolute. It is the tendency to follow and assert our own wills at the expense of God's. Yet when that happens then we have failed the temptation.

Nevertheless, even the devil cannot force anyone to take any of his options. He can only suggest and entice us, but he cannot succeed in our lives in way unless we consent. That is the reason when we make up our minds to trust and rely on God, no temptation can move us regardless of its nature. There is no enticement, or even threat that would be too great for us with God on our side. The Apostle Paul speaks to this when he asks:

*"If God **be for us** who (what) can be (prevail) against us?"* **Romans 8:31.**

This paraphrased can be read; "If God **is** with us, what or who can prevail against us?

TEMPTATION IS A FALSE IMAGE INVOLVING ENTICEMENT

Every temptation is a misrepresentation of the real thing. We observe this in how Adam and Eve were given a misrepresentation of supposedly what God had told them. Unfortunately, the devil convinced them that God was working against them. He somehow presented God to them as someone very mean in the way He was relating and dealing with them. It was like He was hiding or withholding some crucial wisdom and other necessary information from them. The tempter told Eve, "You shall not surely die even if you eat the forbidden fruit". In other words, he was telling her there were no serious or even negative consequences whatsoever if she decided to disobey God.

Nothing would really happen to her; in any case, those were just inhibitions in her mind. Seemingly, he then gave them a promise that all would be well; a promise that was by all means false. He insinuated to them that if they ate that forbidden fruit, they would be happier in life than they ever imagined. They would become significant and self-reliant beings as gods themselves. And as gods they would be as secure as they would want. Indeed, from then on Adam desired to be as God; powerful and for that matter powerful in himself. Yet God had clearly warned them that something terrible would happen if they were to disobey Him.

Nonetheless, the devil intimated and convinced then that God's words to them were mere restrictive (threatening) orders to inhibit their rights and abilities to free expression! "You need to be free; free to indulge yourselves anyhow without worrying about God. Be your own persons; be your own gods." He must have told them. Yet, they did not consider that their freedom was not free from the dependency of their choices contingent on God Himself.

Indeed, freedom is never really free because it dependents on our choices that themselves originated with God. That is why our lives ought to have a solid basis on God and His word. Without that even the best of intentions results in corrupt actions. Therefore, freedom in this sense is not to be free from God who guides the righteous, but to be free from self that corrupts everything.

Pretending to be Mr. Nice, who did not want them to miss out on this knowledge, the devil lectured them on how their eyes would be opened to receive all knowledge involving good and evil. They then gave in to this suggestions and thereby committed high treason, which totally corrupted and disoriented their lives. Hence, temptation easily swept them away. The devil had painted a dark picture of God to them, which resulted in their rejecting God. They, therefore, stood there ready to be turned into their own gods! But alas! They were duped. We find that unfortunate scene in Genesis 3 especially verses 4-6:

> *"And the serpent said unto the woman, Ye shall not surely die. For God doth know that in the day ye eat thereof, then your eyes shall be opened, and ye shall be as gods, knowing good and evil. And when the woman saw that the tree was*

*good for food and that it was pleasant to the eyes and a tree to
be desired to make one wise . . ."*

Eve took the initiative of reasoning things out with the devil,
and by that she opened up to and entertained the enticing
thoughts of the enemy. With subtle reasoning the enemy
convinced her that God was not good. "If He were good, how
could He limit you in the manner He has done?" he seemingly
asked Eve. To him God was working against them, because
He did not tell them the whole truth about that tree in the
middle of the garden. There and then doubt arose in her heart
and the tree began appealing to her. She began to imagine
what they were missing. From her obsession with it, she went
ahead and took its fruit regardless of what she knew was
expected of them.

She knew what was right in their particular situation, yet the
desire to find out more about that forbidden fruit made her
begin to see it differently. It is the point where the forbidden
suddenly becomes admirable. No wonder, she saw that the
tree was good for food and pleasant to look at. The tree or its
fruit was indeed edible since God had indicated so. Hence,
that was not a discovery she was making. It was what she
imagined it tasted like, what puzzled her. Hence, she became
transfixed admiring it with new imaginations reinforced by
the enemy's enticement.

Enticement is simply a picture in the mind created or painted
to lure a person into what may necessarily not be appealing to
them. In Christian terms it is a lure to things forbidden by the
nature of God's life. They are counterfeit to His truth and
purpose. They are false images. Thus, being enticed is simply
being instinctively drawn to accept a false or counterfeit
reality. It may look or even feel as real as God's true design or
plan; yet false. Nonetheless, because of such subtlety, some

people claim certain situations as the best choices for them only to realize they were wrong much later.

In fact, that must have been what Eve thought when she made the choice for the forbidden fruit. But it was a false image the enemy had painted for them. It distorted God's true image and gave them a false representation of God. And that false representation resulted in their acquiring a different outlook at God, which made them reject Him. The devil accused God of being dishonest with them. He insinuated to them that God was blocking their way to godhood and limiting their knowledge. He was doing that to hinder their being like Him in the sense of what He knows.

> *For God doth know that in the day ye eat thereof, then **your eyes shall be opened**, and ye shall be as gods, **knowing** good and evil.* **Genesis 3:5**

Satan told them cunningly that God knew, and may be feared that when they would eat that fruit they would become gods themselves. Hence, they began developing a defective image of God. They saw a God who was *fearful* of them; a God who was *a slur, cunning, overbearing, secretive, competitive,* and every negative adjective you can imagine! And that is how the enemy normally deals with us. He works to make us develop untrue images of God.

The Apostle Paul tells Christians not to be ignorant of the devil's tactics. Satan's main aim in all temptation involvements is human downfall; that is, failing God's approval and connection in life. That is where Eve failed when she gave the enemy a listening ear, and then continued to meditate on the devil's falsehood. Sadly, she then opted for the devil's version of things.

Consequently, some people then claim that God is too strict and difficult to please. Others also see Him as a sadist, who enjoys the suffering of humanity. But none of such sentiments are true about God. Those are false images. Yet because of such, I have been asked time and again; how can a *good* God allow such suffering as is rampant in the world?

But such people only associate God with their imagined definition of goodness. Yet, let us not tie God to human goodness. His goodness may not necessarily involve the human perception of goodness. As a matter of fact, His word says His thoughts are not our thoughts and that His ways are higher than ours. Besides, He has not indicated anywhere that His goodness will cause automatic good on all mankind. Whatever happens to mankind depends on their choices, or choices of those over them. We are a product of our choices.

Thus, people should stop blaming God for evil situations and sufferings of mankind. It is the enemy who plays this blame game. To Adam and Eve, he blamed God for not being truthful or straightforward with them. He questioned God's motive in *imposing* what he considered unnecessary *restrictive standing order* on them not to eat from a certain tree. It was the very first time they heard someone question or challenge God's authority and directives.

Seemingly, they liked it; it played well on their common senses, leading to their grand delusion that they could *become gods* themselves. "Has God said . . . ?" Satan asked Eve. This was questioning their knowledge, belief and resolve in what they thought they knew about God. It was intended to cause her to doubt God in the first place. She was supposed to reflect on it and see if He really said anything like that.

Yet we know that God had purposed for them to live, move and have their being in Him. He set Himself to be their sufficiency. They were to live by faith (trust) in and personal experience of Him based on His word, which sufficed them. Through it they were to exist, because all they needed was in the word. Unfortunately, they cast that a side wanting to live by their own knowledge and reasons. They, therefore, ignored God's word and decided to eat from the tree of the knowledge of good and evil. Therein they acquired the knowledge of good and evil fraudulently through disobedience. Then instead of being wiser than they had imagined, it made them afraid of God.

Then the blame game and every confusions set in. They fled and hid themselves from God, for they had stepped off of His grace-sufficiency. They had opted to begin running their own lives wrapped up within their senses realm. By that they fell from God's grace and became unjust, degraded and accursed by their rebellion against the divine Will. The temptations they battled within that sense sphere were not few; revealing that temptations are much more vigorous within the soul's (sense) realm than otherwise.

Hence, when they accepted a **false** image everything else changed. False images always create false impressions and expectations and that is what Adam and Eve ended up with. Their understanding of the person of God changed completely. All of a sudden they saw God in a different light; as an enemy secretly working against them. But somehow, they presumed to have received that information credibly and in good time. No wonder, the forbidden fruit began appealing to them.

The tree had always been there, but it never appealed to Eve in any way until her selfishness drew her to it. Then while there she was enticed with external suggestions about it. Then she took keen interest on it and you can't imagine what she saw; a delightful tree! Then without thinking twice her lust drew her away and she was enticed! She was stuck between *self-will* and God's *will*. Unfortunately, she chose *self* and that is what we all do when we yield to temptations.

Indeed, in every temptation there is always that element of independence. We desire to be our own persons to do as we please. This is usually wrapped up in the false assumptions that freedom means to be in a state of being unregulated. Then we begin struggling with questions like is God relevant for my life? Is He even necessary? Why must we obey Him and is He really who He claims to be? Does He mean what He says? Can we trust Him? Why should He be the moral authority over us? Why should we not just choose our own lifestyles and preferences without having to worry about Him? Especially people with an intellectual leaning tend to go this route quite easily.

Hence, we see that yielding to temptation is simply choosing self or choosing to operate independent of God. It means we choose self-will and operate from a false image of ourselves; of God and of others. Yet clearly, a false image always leads to regrets; it is contrary to God's design and plans for human welfare.

A CASE EXAMPLE

Jerusamy was a strong choir member and a youth leader in her church. She had been instrumental in keeping a strong and lively youth group in that church, and everyone seemed to like her. She had organized and helped many of the young women get into their marriages. In fact, she participated in most of those weddings in one way or the other, and everyone was looking forward to the day she would walk down the aisle herself. But secretly she was battling unknown forces inside her. She had never had a real boyfriend although people presumed she did.

As a youth leader it appeared she was on top of things, but somehow young men were not showing much interest in her. That secretly bothered her somewhat; she secretly wondered what was wrong with her. All around her, even girls her juniors were getting married, yet she was just there. What was it about her that was not right; why were young men bypassing her to pick up others? Those seemed to be questions she had no answers to and they bothered her a lot. As a matter of fact, she was craving for someone to love her but no one seemed to notice. She desperately wanted to belong to someone. Remember this was long before the smartphone era.

"Why can't any man show interest in me; do I lack anything?" She once quipped to a friend.

Shortly afterwards, she unexpectedly fell in love with one of her brother's workmates. She was alone at home when her brother walked in with a friend he met at work. He had just gotten employed in a new company and met this Christian friend, who wanted to borrow some worship CDs from him. Jerusamy received them well, and her brother introduced them to each other. He then left them in the living room, as he went into his room to bring the worship CDs.

Left to themselves, Jerusamy and the visitor shortly chit chatted about this and that, nothing specific. But something unexpectedly worked between them. There was an attraction between them and they secretly fell in love. Unbeknown to everyone else, she then started visiting him secretly.

Nonetheless, eventually it came to light what was happening. Then her parents talked to her about developing proper relationship and pursuing marriage the right way, if it was what was in her heart. But by then she was very indifferent to them, claiming she was an adult who could decide for herself.

Their pastor was informed and he too, counseled with her for a while. Yet it seemed she had made up her mind; she refused to stop seeing the man. Eventually she eloped with him without a wedding, against all the matured advice of the adults and all who knew her. She claimed that that was what she felt led to do.

All this happened so fast, just in a matter of few months. Later on as she began to settle down in her so-called marriage, she discovered some bitter truths about her "husband". He was an unstable man, who never kept a job for long. He had been married twice before. He deserted one wife with a child while the second one ran a way, citing his unfaithfulness and mistreatments. She further discovered that he was even in an ongoing relationship with a neighbor's daughter, who worked at a nearby grocery store.

Notwithstanding, she found herself in a "marriage" she had presumed was her best decision, but which was slowly turning into a nightmare. It was a false image from the very beginning, yet she refused to see it as such. She unwisely rushed into it unnecessarily refusing to listen to anyone.

TEMPTATIONS ARE MAKE-BELIEVE

Temptations are make-believe. They make one convince themselves that something is what it really isn't. The story of Jerusamy related above is a classic example. She convinced herself that her brother's new friend really loved her. She must have projected how life with him would have been wonderful. It is reported in some quarter that she had claimed he was the best thing that ever happened to her. But only until the reality began to dawn on her. We know what it turned out to be!

Mostly, in temptations you really never fully get what you bargained for. From the start you begin by imagining and working from presumptions how a particular option would benefit you. You imagine the wonderful effects it might bring to you or what you stand to gain; the *prospect of personal gain*. This personal gain factor usurps God's place in us and we quickly embrace the opportunities of apprehending that gain. We then only think in terms of our benefits or the joys or fulfillment we stand to draw or gain by taking those particular options.

That is where Adam and Eve were; they were after gain and in that case, gain for themselves. They did not care the least whether their gain – *becoming god* – would have affected God in any way. They did not care the least whether they infringed on God's Will or not. The only thing that actually mattered to them then was what they stood to gain.

Temptations always come in ways that deny or disguise the negative consequences. In them you never get the whole picture, especially with regards to consequences that might follow. It is always marked by the false belief that we will never suffer any consequences. You will be bargaining only on the half grounds of gain (the benefits), not realizing the hidden (unspoken) consequences lurking in the shadows. As a result people jump headlong into situations without any consideration at all, only thinking in terms of their immediate enjoyment or gains. They never consider anyone else, but themselves. They are convinced that their presumptions are true. This is why I say it is *make-believe*.

Back to Eden, Eve saw and believed that the tree of the knowledge of good and evil could make them wise. She convinced herself it could totally change their lives for the better. But it was an illusion; a make-believe. Yet she did not realize it then; she was self-deceived because all **make-believe** results into *self-deception*. Accordingly, when we are only concerned with, and are governed by the prospects of our selfish gains or enjoyments, then we should take note that we are treading the paths to self-deception and eventual failure.

An example here is the famous prophet Balaam son of Bosor, who though a prophet of sorts intentionally forsook the right way and went astray for love of **gain** and *dignity*. The prophet turned into a *hireling*. He accepted to be hired to do ministry, though without a specific call from God to that specific thing. Sadly, that is even the state of affairs today in some Christian circles. Some of our so-called ministries are made up of people, who jumped on to the bandwagon of *ministry* simply with their eyes on some kind of gain; mostly things that answer to the here and now.

CHAPTER THREE

WHERE DO TEMPTATIONS COME FROM?

Temptations come from our own desires based on our freedom of choice. God told Adam and Eve they could *freely* eat of every tree in the garden except one. Freely eat . . . that was it; it gave them the freedom of choice and with it came the temptation. Temptations occur in what are generally the normal life experiences or situations we face every day. Some come to us as a result of our environments, while some are imposed on us by others: Friends, family members, fellow church members; at the grocery stores, at the malls, at bookstores, at work, driving down the roads and so on. But they all have one thing in common; they give us opportunities for choice making either for righteousness or otherwise.

For example, Tom a newly married young executive of a certain dot com company was an elder is his church and knew all about God's love. He had a date with his wife Shirley that evening, and when he left his office it started to rain lightly. The traffic was light, but somewhat slow. His thoughts, as he was driving home, were mostly on his date with his wife. However, suddenly appeared this reckless driver who was weaving his way in between other cars with loud music blaring from his stereos. He came right behind Tom and then he squeezed his way into the next lane. Then abruptly before Tom knew it, the guy tried cutting right in front of him and you cannot imagine what happened. He hit Tom's car. "Oh

41

no," bawled Tom getting out of his car in the rain. "What is wrong with you man, can't you use your head; where were you rushing to? How can you do this to me?" Tom asked angrily.

The other fellow also got out of his car asking Tom, "are you all right man; are you all right?" But Tom felt like squeezing the life out of him. How could he do such a *stupid thing*? There it was set before him to make a choice either for righteousness or otherwise. He could abuse, curse and yell the much he wanted or he could quiet himself by the grace of God as they waited for the police.

KEY FACTORS IN ANY TEMPTATION

"There hath no temptation taken you but such as is common to man..." **1 Corinthians 10:13a**

The Apostle Paul in this verse informs us that there is no temptation that is an exclusive experience. All temptations are common. What you may be undergoing now, someone else has undergone or would be undergoing. In other words, there is nothing new under the sun. Some things may appear new to those undergoing them, but the Bible says they are common to humanity. This means nothing anyone may be undergoing is new. No one is alone in whatever situations they may be faced with. Someone somewhere has undergone or are also undergoing the same things. As such, take heart and continue trusting God.

Paul says, "There hath no **temptation** taken **you** but such as is common to man. . ." From this we see that there are two key factors in every temptation set up. These are:

i.   **You** – the tempted person and
ii. **Temptation** (Something) - the enticement

You (the tempted person) are usually tempted about or with **something.** Let's consider these two factors in more details.

THE 'YOU' FACTOR IN TEMPTATIONS

- 'You' (the person) play a big role in any temptation set-up; without you there can be no temptation in your case. Every temptation occurs in your now or your present moment. In other words, temptation is usually present tense and as such you cannot be tempted in absentia.

- 'You' must be an **independent decision-maker** to be tempted. As long as you entirely depend on others to decide for you, you will never know what temptation is! For instance, an infant who is dependent on its parents does not know what it means to be tempted until it begins to make its own decisions. This means, a person who cannot think properly and independently cannot be tempted. Their conduct is determined for them by others, and hence they cannot have any sense of temptation.

- 'You' are not expected to be infallible in the face of temptations, not even God expects that of you. Human beings can fail, err or make mistakes. Therefore, it is unnecessary to be hard on yourself if you happen to fail. Don't blame yourself, it is just a test; learn from it and move on.

- 'You' should be aware that God is fully aware of our frailty and it does not surprise Him when we do something wrong. Thus, do not sit on your failure; God is waiting to give you another chance to the right hand of fellowship with Him through the means of confession.

- 'You' can, therefore, choose to let God help you get back on to your feet, if fail the temptations. He will grant you forgiveness, and thereby bring you back into right fellowship with him.

- 'You' can initiate that forgiveness process by responding to His grace immediately you fail. The first step in being restored to fellowship with Him is to freely acknowledge, and accept that you have indeed failed. Then confess and repent of it as soon as possible. No matter what you did, God will fully and freely forgive and restore you if you sincerely confess it.

This is the message we have heard of Him and declare unto you that God loves us and went into great lengths of giving His own Son to die for us. Why would He not forgive our sins now when Jesus has already shed His blood for the same! God is faithful and just, so His word tells us. He will forgive any sins anytime; run to Him and Christ's precious blood, which He shed on Calvary's cross will cleanse them all. That is how to get a right standing with God once again.

Some people do well in their walks with God, only until they suddenly fail temptations and then they think that is the end. But I am here to encourage you that that is not the case. Rebound and make a comeback to grace involvements with God, if you happen to fail. Doing that will set your heart right again; it is what is expected of every child of God, who have violated His will. You should be ready to make a comeback, because God is always ready for such eventualities to restore people to His unbroken fellowship.

THE ENTICEMENT FACTOR IN TEMPTATIONS

The nature of "the enticement" in temptation is that:
- It will be something common to you; usual, normal, or regular.

- It will be something in your line of thoughts.
- It will be in your general dealings
- It will be readily available to you, even within your reach.
- It will be easy to do or be involved with
- It will be beneficial to you or appear so
- It will appear to satisfy your particular desires
- It will be portrayed as able to prove something about you

TEMPTATION IS USUALLY SOMETHING COMMON TO YOU

"And when the tempter came to Him, he said if thou be the son of God, command that these stones be made bread." Mathew 4:3.

The "bait" used in tempting Jesus in His first temptation was 'stones'. The Tempter told Him ". . . Command that these stones be made bread". Stones were readily available to Him in all directions and that is what was used to tempt Him. This portrays that temptation is usually with something common to and readily available to you. Jesus was tempted with something within His reach and a common necessity - bread. You will always be tempted with something you are exposed to and readily available or needful to you.

TEMPTATION IS USUALLY SOMETHING IN YOUR LINE OF THOUGHTS

Second, temptations will be with things within your line of thoughts. For instance, a local bicycle repairer cannot wake up one morning tempted to go rob a bank! That will not be the case; if he is to be tempted, it will have to do with something within the sphere of his life and his line of thoughts. That means he might be tempted to steal some bicycle spare parts, or defraud his customers, but not to go rob a bank. Neither can a simple housewife be tempted to go on the highways and carjack motorist. That would be something far removed from her line of thoughts and lifestyle, unless someone else introduces her to such a venture.

Even in Jesus in Mathew 4:1-7, we find words like: Man shall not live by bread alone, but by every **word** that proceedeth out of the mouth of **God** . . . , taketh him up into the **holy** city, setteth him on . . . the **temple,** thou shalt not tempt the **Lord** thy **God,** shown all the **kingdom, worship** the Lord thy **God**. These were the things in Jesus' line of thought; the word of God, God, holy, temple, Lord, Kingdom, and worship. They are what were used to tempt Him. This bespeaks that you will only be tempted with things common to you and in your line of thoughts, or within your circle of influence or dealings.

TEMPTATION IS SOMETHING EASY TO DO OR ENGAGE IN

It is usually something you can do or indulge (engage) in easily. It is within your power and ability to efficiently and easily do. That was what Mr. Godfrey Rayah a businessman of international repute, experienced on his business trip to one of the western capitals. As he was relaxing in his hotel lounge waiting for a business friend, a beautiful lady approached him wanting to know if he needed company. She was available and ready to be of service to him, if that was something he could opt for. "What makes you think I need company ma'am?" inquired Godfrey.

"I see you are alone here and I know you can use and appreciate my services," replied the lady.

Somehow, it did not take long before Mr. Rayah found himself attracted to that woman. Before he knew it, the lady had won his affections and momentarily threw him off guard. He then invited her to his hotel room. While they were walking to his room he felt like telling her he was a Christian, but somehow he felt awkward about it. When they reached his room the lady did not even wait; she grabbed him and started kissing him passionately while trying to remove his jacket.

His heart began to pound so hard with his hands sweating profusely. He was battling in his mind over what he was about to do. He was overwhelmed with passion and at the point of letting go, yet he knew what was expected of him. But just then his phone rang and he answered it. It was his business friend who had heard he was in town and swung-by to see him. That was it; that call is what broke the spell of that lady over Mr. Rayah. The point here is that temptations are things you can do easily.

There he was thousands of miles away from his family, his fellow church members and business associates; no one would have known what he would have done on his business trip had he decided to sleep with that lady. You see this was something readily available to and very easy for him to do. It was something he could have done and gotten over with. Yet doing that would have been sinning against God, his wife and all the people who love him. But God rescued him in the nick of time; at the worst point of his temptation.

This was certainly an embarrassing situation to Mr. Rayah, but in everyday life we are all faced up with such choices in differing scenarios. The opportunities to secretly do things that dishonor our God are always with us in abundance. We are all capable of turning our backs on God as we indulge in some of our fleshly desires. To some people it is an attraction to pornography or other sexual sins, or drugs and so forth. But the choices lie with each one of us.

Even Jesus in the wilderness was tempted with things He could easily do. "Turn these stones into bread," Satan told Him. That was a very easy task; He could do it in an instant. Satan came to Him when He was at His lowest point in an empty stomach, though full of power and the Holy Spirit. He had all the powers at His disposal, but lacked something to eat. If He had liked, just at His word or touch those stones would have turned into bread! That is the reason He was tempted along that line, with things He could easily, efficiently and readily do. He was capable of doing it, but He was under no necessity to do so.

Back to Genesis 3, we see Eve struggling with the temptation of whether to eat the fruit or not. It was something very easy for her to do, just pluck and eat and unfortunately she did and the consequences are known to all of us. In fact, it is the ease with which some things can be done what makes people plunge into them without a second thought! That is how it goes. Temptations are usually things we can do easily. You will rarely be tempted with things you can never easily do or indulge in.

TEMPTATIONS PORTRAYED AS GOOD OR BENEFICIAL TO YOU

Temptation is usually with *something*, which by all human judgments is good and is desirable. It comes as a means that will help or enhance something within you. Reflecting on Jesus' temptations, the devil seemed to have told Him; why are you starving yourself to death? Help yourself, change this situation around; turn these stones into bread so you can eat and be strengthened. It was a sensible talk. In fact, Jesus would have benefited a lot from the acts proposed by the devil. The point here is that you do not yield to temptations so the devil or someone else benefits. Whatever you do, you are the beneficiary and that is the catch. It is all centered on *you*.

It has been pointed out that an accountant who defrauds his company of finances only in the majority of the cases does it for himself. It is rear to hear of someone who stole or defrauded money and deposited it in someone else's account where he had no interests at all! The temptation is always about our self-interest (good) and benefit. Even Jesus turning the stones into bread was all for His own benefit. And that is not something bad by any human standards! If you stand to benefit or enjoy the situation then it appeals to your weaknesses, particularly when portrayed as good. Hence, temptation always appears as good and desirable undertakings able to thrill or benefit us.

> *And when the woman saw that the tree was good for food and that it was pleasant to the eyes and a tree to be desired to make one wise ...*" **Genesis 3:6**

Eve saw that the tree they had been restricted from eating was then looking good. But God in His wisdom had prohibited their eating its fruits regardless of how it appeared. No wonder, some men caught in adultery, often claim that they were overcome by the beauty of the women they got involved with. Yet, as a matter of fact; looks can be deceptive.

That became true in Eve's case; by human reasoning, she deduced that that tree was good anyway, even if God forbade it. Not only that, but to her it seemed to be a great source of admiration as it was *pleasant to the eyes*. It was beautiful to look at. Prohibited things generally appeal to our desires. Just the thought of them makes us imagine what great pleasures we stand to derive from them!

Hence, to Eve that tree was desirable to make one wise. She supposedly considered that eating its fruits could endow them with wisdom unbeknown; some hidden wisdom. Likely, that was a move in the right direction for them; a profitable move then. And that is where most of us have problems; good things, good feelings, good expectations, good desires and so forth.

Nonetheless, God does not intend for anyone to live only on the basis of their own *good* intentions or feelings. People often ask, "Oh, how can such a good feeling be wrong?" But if God prohibits it then it is wrong.

TEMPTATION CAN SATISFY IMMEDIATE DESIRES

It is important to understand that temptation will indeed satisfy an immediate appetite, urge or desire but shortly. Sadly, that is what continues to attract some people into sin; the fact that temptation is meeting their certain needs or desires. Clearly, some of such appetites or desires are legitimate. Except that the temptation wants us to fulfill them illegitimately. This means the problem is not the appetites, but how we take care of them.

Jesus' hunger after forty day's fasting was legitimate; it was not evil to be hungry. But the devil wanted Him to employ unlawful means of meeting that need. Even, our sexual needs are not wrong in themselves, but if we try meeting them using our neighbor's spouse or someone not our spouses then it is sin. That is what temptations move us to do. They come as means of meeting such particular needs through unlawful means, promising us happiness, significance and security acquired our own way.

Put another way, inordinate desires always default to inordinate means of gratifying them. Yes, there is a feeling of fulfillment or enjoyment in accepting temptations, whatever they may be. But it is usually inordinate and short lived, leaving you craving for more.

TEMPTATIONS PROVE OR DISAPPROVE "SOMETHING" ABOUT US

Temptations come to prove some point either positive or negative about us. To Jesus the first temptation was to prove He was really the Son of God by turning stones into bread! "If you are the son of God turn these stones into bread," the devil told Him. The suggestions here were intended to dissuade Him from the known fact that He was indeed the Son of God. He had just come from the River Jordan where His Father had verbally expressed great pleasure in Him by the descent of the Holy Spirit. God had indeed declared Him the Son of His great pleasure. Yet in the temptation the enemy began to challenge that very fact demanding He proves it if He really was the Son of God. Temptation questions and casts shadow on God's word about us and pits our wills against His. It comes to have us prove or disapprove "things" about ourselves.

In Jesus' case the devil told Him, *if thou be the Son of God . . .* That was tempting Him to doubt that He was actually God's Son. Satan knew Jesus was the son of God and even Jesus knew it. But Satan had to frame his questions so as to cause Jesus to doubt what He knew very well. The strategy is always to cause doubt on the outset and, if he succeeds there then he succeeds everywhere else. That's why Satan was trying to dissuade Him from holding to His identity as the true Son of the living God. He was questioning the very thing God had declared about Jesus.

And Satan does that with us always, trying to have us prove his suggestions. Even with Eve, the first thing he did was to plant doubt in her mind about God. "Has God said...?" He asked. He wanted to prove to her that what she believed was not exactly what God meant or had said. That is, if it was even said at all!

He is always in the business of trying to prove some things with suggestions like *prove you really love the Lord,* and if you do; how comes you did this and that? Or do you remember how you did . . . some *negative thing.* The point is; shift from whom or what you are in God to Satan's intimidating and incriminating suggestions. It is good he even tried such tactics with Jesus, but he failed because Jesus stood His ground. He knew who He was and He refused to engage in Satan's suggestions to prove Himself.

The proof question did not end with that first temptation; it went on even to the second, where Jesus was to prove that God is true to His word. To find out the Devil told Him to jump from the temple pinnacle.

> And (he, the devil) said unto him, *if thou be the Son of God, cast thyself down: for it is written, He shall give his angels charge concerning thee: and in their hands they shall bear thee up, lest at any time thou dash thy foot against a stone.* **Matthew 4:6**

Jesus was to jump and see if the angels would really be there to catch Him, but He refused to play along. He knew that God's truthfulness does not depend on His jumping or not. God is always true.

Sometimes such temptations come trying to prove things about us through others, or just from our own minds. For instance, to someone with marital problems suggestions like you are really not satisfied or happy in this relationship, will often pop up. Or even others like your partner knows you are not right for them; what are you waiting for. Get out and go look for someone who understands and accepts you. The suggestions try proving that you are not satisfied in your marriage, or that you are not right for your spouse! Or even further that there are people out there who would be more understanding and accepting than your spouse. And often many of us fall for those suggestions.

In other cases, temptations even involve protecting our image (name) or reputation. A teenage daughter of one of the prominent bishops in a certain city, got pregnant while in a Bible College! The Bishop's family did everything to keep that information secret and prevailed upon their daughter to do everything in her powers to save them the embarrassment that would often arise from such situations. To save face in the society, they secretly influenced their daughter to procure an abortion. In a short while, the would-be-embarrassing situation was no more; the pregnancy was gone. The girl was then "free" and ready to go back to her Bible College. Her family's image was purportedly protected from her irresponsible behavior by the act of her procuring an abortion!

TEMPTATIONS INDULGE OUR NATURAL LIFE

Yielding to temptation is simply indulging *self-life, or the natural life*. It is the yielding to doing things our own way and making choices without regards to God. This means, temptation is pegged on the ability to freely make choices on the basis of right and wrong. And selfishness is the root of all wrong choices, springing from *self-will* and *selfish* interests. That is why Christians who live by the natural order have more struggles with temptations than those learning to die daily and let Christ be their life.

It is not that the Lord wants us to deny our nature or that we should be 'senseless', but that such senses should be employed within Him. That is, we must live by Him and in Him move with our senses under His total control and governance. Whenever people live the Christian life based on their natural life; they cannot help struggling and being defeated by the various temptations.

In fact, this is where the tempter intended to bring Jesus; to live by the natural order of thing when he told Him to turn stones into bread. Jesus had spent over one month communicating with His Father in the atmosphere of divine Spirit. Then the devil appeared intending to drag Him out of the Spirit to draw His attention to the physical things. The whole point with the devil was not just the turning of those stones into bread, but the source of that action. You can see the tempter didn't tell Jesus to have His Father supply His needs or to pray to God to turn those stones into bread.

It was all to be from Jesus; it was to be His initiative and action. But such an action was it from *self* or from the Spirit of God! Knowing this trick Jesus refused such an offer countering that man's life is not just the physical existence. He said man does not just live on bread – the physical alone. In other words, man's life is more than just its physical aspects.

The story of Mr. Darly Ndon'ga, an export-import businessman, is a good example in this case of indulging natural life. His work involved dealing in imported merchandise from Dubai ranging from clothing to electronics. One time a lady, a single parent of a seven years old girl, came into his office for consultations wanting to try her hand at the imports business. She had previously worked for an airline industry, but had been laid off then.

Surprisingly the chemistry between them went crazy at first sight and got them into a secret love affairs. But the secrecy did not last long as their affair blossomed into a relationship with Darly flirting with her openly. He started taking her to his Dubai trips and other functions. Sadly, it did not take long before he selfishly abandoned his wife and kids for this single mother! Yet, I am not suggesting that single mothers are evil people; no, I am only pointing out that Darly made bad choices of indulging his selfishness to the detriment of his family.

Falling into temptation, therefore, is simply indulging **self;** yielding to doing things that our flesh desires, and making such choices without considering God or others. It could be the lust of the eye; lust of the flesh or the pride of life, but it is all within self. It always challenges our resolve and belief (knowledge) about our stand for God. No wonder, the apostle Paul says we should take heed when we think we are standing lest we fall.

Overall, temptation is always with something:
- Common to you; usual, normal, or regular.
- In your line of thoughts and desires.
- In your general dealings
- Readily available to you, even within your reach.
- Easy to do or be involved with
- Beneficial to you or appears so
- Able to shortly satisfy your particular desires
- Able to prove something about you
- That challenges our belief and knowledge of God and cause us to doubt Him

---

CHAPTER FOUR

KEEN LOOK AT JESUS' TEMPTATIONS

THE FIRST TEMPTATION

"Then was Jesus led up of the spirit into the wilderness to be tempted of the devil. And when he had fasted forty days and forty nights, he was afterward hungry. **And when the tempter came to him, he said, If thou be the Son of God, command that these stones be made bread.** *But he answered and said, It is written, Man shall not live by bread alone, but by every word that proceedeth out of the mouth of God."* **Matthew 4:1-4.**

This was the first temptation where Jesus was to express His *Self-Will* or act independent from God. Seemingly, there was no logical reason for Him to starve when He had all the powers. Satan considering that He was hungry gave Him the option to satisfy that need. He told Him to turn stones into bread with a view to eating. And from eating He would naturally receive strength that would help Him continue engaging with His Father, and eventually achieve *His* purpose. That was seemingly a reasonable approach, but Jesus declined it. He did not come with His own personal purpose, except the will of His Father.

No wonder, He opted to be a servant that He might learn obedience. In other words, He was being tempted to be independent. Satan was tempting Him based upon natural circumstances and inclinations to step out ahead of His time. This was not so much about doing some obviously sinful thing, but simply to get Him to make decisions independent of His Father. It was a chance to act from *self* instead of acting from the Father in whom He was. If He would have done so, it would have shown that He trusted Himself more than He trusted God.

That is what the devil did with Adam and Eve. Satan always wants those he tempts to act independent of God; to initiate something a part from God. This is what he wanted Jesus to do; to show that He was independent minded or willed for that matter. But instead Jesus proved His total dependence on His Father. The devil was telling Him to *serve self,* but He had nothing for *self; self-consideration, self-pleasing, self-determination, self-promotion, self-arguments, self-desires, selfish interests* and so on. To Him it was always, "not my will, but thine . . ." or "I delight to do thy will O my God."

The tempter expected Him as the Son of God to invoke and use His special and privileged position to serve *self;* to pamper His earthly appetites and minister to His immediate physical needs, but He refused. In fact, He answered the devil not as the Son of God but as a man. He took the position of a man and answered that man shall not live by bread alone. He turned the tables on the devil who came wanting to engage Him as the Son of God, but only found the son of man.

Notice that He did not answer Satan that Son of God does not eat bread or something. No; He said that MAN shall not live by bread (the natural strength) alone. In other words, He said that mankind was not created to live on the physical realm only. Human life is not just about the physical aspect of it. A person's whole life is more than just the physical; it should involve their need to live by every word of God. Mankind was created for God. This kind of talk began to confuse the devil. First, he came to confront Jesus as the Son of God and he met Jesus speaking as the son of man. Then this Jesus the man, who should have been hungry to death, seemingly did not seem to care much about food. That got Satan confused, he could not understand how.

You see his first temptation on both Adam and Jesus was the same; it was about acting independent of God in eating something. To Adam – the temptation was to *eat* from the tree of knowledge of good and evil; while to Jesus – it was to turn stones into bread with a view to *eating*. But Jesus stood His ground as a man, or son of man who lived by every word from God's mouth. That realization took the wind off the devil's sail, because he had not expected to meet such a person. Especially, one who turned everything back to God!

In this case, the devil tempted Him to rely on His own ability and sufficiency even for legitimate and necessary things like food, but He refused. He did not employ His miraculous powers or privileged position to serve His personal needs in any manner as to disprove His connection to and dependence on God. He declined to *serve His own Will* and this attempt by the devil to sideline Him failed. The enemy was stunned.

His earlier attempts with other people had been successful whenever he passed through the medium of their bodily appetites, or their physical desires. Yet on this occasion he met a man whose bodily appetites or senses did not control Him! He found out that Jesus could not be manipulated or appealed to, through His desires. Indeed, he found out that Jesus kept talking about things that are written, and about God. Hence, the devil decided to change tact and speak to Him from that vantage point involving what was written. That then leads us to the next temptation.

THE SECOND TEMPTATION

"Then the devil taketh him up into the holy city, and setteth him on a pinnacle of the temple, And saith unto him, If thou be the Son of God, cast thyself down: for it is written, He shall give his angels charge concerning thee: and in their hands they shall bear thee up, lest at any time thou dash thy foot against a stone. Jesus said unto him, It is written again, Thou shalt not tempt the Lord thy God." **Matthew 4:5-7**

Having failed on the first attempt, the devil seeing Jesus insisting on God's word decided to also bring in some scriptures. He thought he was going to get Jesus on His own ground; the word of God. That is what he did with the first Adam, wherein he asked hath God said? Although this time round he did not question what God had said. He affirmed it but cunningly. With this he wanted to convince Jesus that they were on the same page agreeing on what God had said.

He does that with us always, whispering to us that even the word says, *"there is none righteous no not one. And there is none that doeth good, no not so much as one!"* Everyone does this once in a while. Furthermore, God understands. God knows you are flesh and blood, or that you are just human. He can take it further by telling you that even some ministers do this or that; simply trying to give you comfort in sin.

It is on this principle of quoting scriptures that he came and told Jesus to jump down the Temple pinnacle. His intention with this was Jesus' *self-exaltation* and fame. Satan was reminding Jesus that as the Son of God, even the angels were on standby for any of His acts. Especially, if He could execute it there in Jerusalem, the holy city that was close to every Jew's heart, then what a wonder that was to be. Indeed, Jerusalem was the best place for such a mighty public performance of inaugurating Himself as the new prophet everyone had been waiting for. Jumping down the temple pinnacle would have served Him well in gaining recognition and making a name, thereby becoming famous.

Thus, jumping down the Temple pinnacle was not just about the jumping, or even the supposed angels who would have come to His rescue; it was more of the subsequent impact it would have had on the *Jerusalemites*. Satan meant for Him to *seek self-exaltation* and let people openly recognize who He really was. Why was He hiding His real identity, yet He also knew who He was and His mission!

He knew that for about four hundred years, there had been no acclaimed prophet based on people's understanding then. Their traditions had had it that the coming Messiah would do wonderful supernatural signs to arouse the attention of the Jews and prove His identity. And nothing could have been better placed for Him to begin such supernatural undertakings than jumping from the Temple pinnacle right there in Jerusalem. He would have gathered unprecedented following right there and then.

People were eagerly awaiting the Messiah. Thus, He only needed to dramatically reveal that He was He. He knew He was the Messiah, what was wrong in His coming out with such a pronouncement! He only needed a good chance, like the one He was being offered then to announce His arrival. Oh, what crowds He could have pulled! Even the Jerusalem lays-about and passersby would have joined it! He would have become an instant celebrity, and the fame of it would have spread far and wide. What a good opportunity Jesus had for starting His ministry so powerfully! Yet, He rejected those kinds of suggestions and overcame the temptation.

He rejected that avenue of announcing His arrival as the Messiah so as to be acclaimed and received by the people. He knew it would not serve God's purpose of changing the people's hearts, which was His mission. Rather, He opted to declare the truth to them bit by bit (precept upon precept), because truth received and acted upon sets people free. He wanted them free, first of all from *themselves* and their traditionally patterned notions.

They had expected He would necessarily free them from the Roman rule. But the freedom He brought begins with the individual persons. Yet that was far from their expectations and desires then. They wanted external things and factors to change first, presuming that would have liberated them. They just wanted Him to overthrow the Roman rulers and then they would have rallied behind Him as their hero. But to some of them, seemingly Jesus did not want to be a hero.

Nevertheless, the thought of being great or even the slightest desire for it did not occur to Him. He did not think it anything to hold on to being equal with God, let alone being famous on earth. He had just emptied Himself of the most grandeur position in heaven, what was any position worth on earth? Yet, in Genesis when Eve heard they would become gods by eating the forbidden fruit; she immediately distrusted God. Then the inordinate desire for God's power and glory overwhelmed her, and sadly she did not think twice; she went ahead and ate the fruit.

Even Jesus would have become a great public spectacle had He accepted to go the devil's way. But He refused to seek fame in that manner. He did not come for fame. Moreover, He knew it was not the Father's Will for Him just to attract people to Himself without purposefully and clearly showing them the Father. He had been appointed to come reveal the Father and His knowledge to humanity.

He did not come just to be famous, or simply for people to see Him; they were to see the Father in Him. He also knew that the time for that kind of an act was not yet and so He put aside the apparent requests to perform. Not only did the people want Him to perform for them, but there was also a lingering desire with such upcoming leaders to appear great among the scholars and religious leaders of then. It was one of the rarest opportunities to be someone great or someone to be looked up to in that society.

People everywhere, especially the religious leaders craved for such opportunities. Yet Jesus here rejected such an opportunity; refusing *self*-exaltation, or even to allow the people to exalt Him. He rather exalted and glorified God. Still later in His ministry when people pressured Him to act on His own to accept to be their King; He flatly refused. He knew that seeking recognition of men, of the world or self or the praise thereof was to grieve the Lord of glory.

In this temptation He was confronted with a misinterpretation of God's word, but He saw right through it. That purported word, the devil quoted focused so much on His supposed *self-importance*. Yet, He was and is always important; it was nothing He was to allow to cloud out His mission of doing His Father's Will. In fact, it is recorded that He did not count equality with God as anything to cling to.

Hence, to Him His importance was not an issue; it was not even the Father's specific and direct word for Him then. With such a strong stand that temptation disguised in scriptural quotations flopped. But today how many of us can resist such an offer to become famous!

THE THIRD TEMPTATION

"Again, the devil taketh him up into an exceeding high mountain, and sheweth him all the kingdoms of the world, and the glory of them, And saith unto him, All these things will I give thee, If thou will fall down and worship me. Then saith Jesus unto him, Get thee hence, Satan: for it is written, Thou shalt worship the Lord thy God, and him only shalt thou serve" **Matthew 4:8-10**.

When the two previous temptations failed the devil then pulled out his very best, which he had reserved for the last. This was the **power and glory** idea. He was ready to usher Jesus into power and glory but through compromise. This was special because it is the idea that astounded Adam just on the very first encounter without much ado. Power and glory usually appeal to people and Satan presumed it would somehow appeal to Jesus too.

The temptation here was that if He would have worshipped the tempter, He would have been given the kingdoms of the world and the power to control everything. It was the temptation to love the world and the things in it. It was the offer of materialism and the glory of power resulting in the *control* of the world systems. The devil demanded to be worshipped. "Worship me and I will give you the control of life and all that goes with it," seemed to be what he was saying. He insinuated that it only took worshipping him and all could be Jesus'. He was privy to Jesus' ultimate purpose of worship in fulfilling His Father's will.

Yet that involved going to the Cross, which though a painful experience was the surest test of true love and obedience to God. That is why Satan burst into the scene determined to subvert that ultimate worship by offering Jesus an alternative way.

"You do not need to go all that long and cruel way of the Cross your Father has purposed for you. I will spare you all that pain and suffering, but still give you the kingdoms and glory. It is simple, just bow down and worship me and that is it. Is there a better deal than this?" the devil seemingly told Him.

But Jesus refused, because He had insight that whom you worship; Him you will serve. *Thou shalt **worship** the Lord thy God and him only shalt thou **serve.*** If He would have worshipped the devil then He would have been bound to serve him, yet that was not His mission in life.

The Bible implies that Satan knew what the Cross of Jesus would do to him and his kingdom, so he had to do everything possible to dissuade Jesus from going that route. Hence, he offered Him a shortcut – a cross-less way into the kingdom and glory. But thank goodness Jesus refused. Even when He was shown the riches, the glory and power of the earthly kingdoms; He still could not be persuaded to disobey God. He intentionally refused them because He understood that one can gain the whole world and eventually lose his life. All the material wealth without God is vanity.

He understood that materialism or power is not the real answer to the meaning of life. Thus, He rejected it all; recognition and praise of men, and He rather chose to go the way of the Cross. Satan had intended to give Him the glory and power through compromise (back door), but He refused and gained it through obedience; even obedience unto death! Then God vindicated Him by raising Him from the dead and uniting Him with His fullness of eternal glories.

He made Himself of **no reputation** that His need of dependence on God might take precedence. You know people have either good or bad reputations, but Jesus decided to have none; no reputation at all! Without a reputation He did not have anything to defend or worry about. He did not have to worry about what people would say or think about Him, or His ministry and so forth.

As such, when offered these external factors He rejected them because He knew very well that true meaning of life comes from God. Furthermore, the Bible teaches that life (eternal) was already bound up in Him. Then looking back to His first temptation He understood that human life is more than the things He was being offered. With His deep understanding of the Father, His temptations increased His love for and dependence on God. He thereby, refused to bow to the devil knowing very well that Satan's offers have no guarantees. They are illegitimate as he offers things that don't belong to him in the first place.

Largely, we learn that these temptations don't just come once. They are recurring phenomena; what we go through today does not pass away forever. If you are tempted to lust today, it does not mean you will never be tempted along that line again. You will definitely meet it again, even if in a different way.

Hence, you must not say you have already overcome certain temptations once and for all. Oh no, somehow you will find yourself facing them again and again. That simply means you will never out-grow temptations; there is no place (plateau) in this life you will reach where you cannot be tempted. It is foolhardy to presume you have won a certain spiritual battle forever. Temptations are never won once for all. You will often find ourselves fighting over familiar grounds and have to learn your lessons once again.

Typically, these three temptations were aimed at self: Self-motivation, Self-preservation, and Self-recognition; Self-pity, Self-achievement, and Self-sufficiency. Yet Jesus had given up everything, including His rights to being equal with God; thus, He was not governed by *self* in any way or form. Consequently, these temptations never lured Him into disobedience to His Father.

CHAPTER FIVE

HOW TO FACE TEMPTATIONS

Our responses in temptation situations determine whether we overcome or are overcome. The easiest way to fail temptations is to be ignorant of the devil's tactics, and thereby react instead of responding appropriately to situations as they unfold. Sometimes people even fail to realize the difference between responding and reacting to situations. Response simply means to answer or give favorable attention to; whereas reaction is to spontaneously act in opposition to, more so on an emotional streak.

Some studies have shown that we are more likely to overcome situations by proper response to them than by reacting. Godly expectation is that such responses should be informed by what I call SPARE; an acronym for a life that is:

- ❋ **S**aturated with God's word
- ❋ **P**rayerful
- ❋ **A**ttentive and vigilant in God
- ❋ **R**ejoicing at all times in the gracious work of God in us
- ❋ **E**nduring - as a good soldier of Jesus Christ

Thus, temptations are easy to face with a SPARE life. Let me simplistically explain how to get the SPARE life beginning with the letter S.

S – Saturate your life with the word, and presence of God long before temptations come. That means you must live dedicated

---

to Him fully. In doing that, you learn much about God's life in the human soul to the point that you understand temptations to be transient. You also learn about yourself – your vulnerabilities and dispositions.

Therefore, give heed to and live by every word of God. It is what Paul refers to as letting the word of God dwell richly in you. Eventually, that word will rule your heart and thereby guide your life. Hence, when temptations come, you will already be soaked in His word and there is nothing that can defeat you with God on your side.

> *Blessed is the man who walks not in the counsel of the ungodly, nor stands on the way of sinners, nor sits on the seat of the scornful. But his delight is in the law of the Lord, and in it, He does meditate day and night.* **Psalm 1:1-2**

But without proper grounding in the word, you will find yourself operating from your own wisdom that is the ground of many distractions and defeats.

P – Pray with prayers both private and personal, in the spirit and in understanding. Pray and practice God's counsel daily, because there is nothing more portent to the work of the enemy than prayerfulness. As you pray and submit to Christ, your spirit will begin to soar with Him. Jesus said that the spirit indeed is always willing, but the flesh is generally weak. The way to be strengthened usually is to spend quality time with Him. The answer to victory in temptations lies in your relationship with God on a personal level (Ephesians 6:17-18). This is cultivated long before such eventualities of temptations appear. Note that victory is a result not a single act in the process of temptation. If you want the result, commit to the process long before. This is the reason SPARE life is very important.

A – Attend to situations and circumstances around you in a sober and vigilant manner - because your adversary the devil goes around looking for someone to devour. Do not be presumptuous or take things for granted. Try finding out the meaning and purpose of every situation you may be faced with. And don't let this slip off your mind that all things work together for the good to them that love God who are the called according to His purpose. And you are one of those called according to His purpose. Indeed, your God will cause all things to work together for your good. Thus, remain steadfastly trusting Him, because He never fails. (Romans 8:28, 1 Peter 5:6-8).

R – Rejoice in the Lord always, not that you are tempted but because He is your Father and He has your good at heart. James tells us to count it all joy when we are tempted. One reason for this is because temptations do not come to finish nor to embitter, but to better us. That is simply a call to a positive frame of mind by which you will be able withstand anything life may throw at you.

E – Endure as a good soldier of Jesus Christ. That is, bear situations with patience and constancy maintaining dignity and integrity. Always remembering that the trial of your faith works God's purposes in you (2 Timothy 2:3). Although sometimes we do not understand or know what God might be doing, but even in such cases we must still trust Him. Whatever it is, His purposes for us will turn out good.

OVERCOMING TEMPTATIONS

Someone may now wonder why the need to overcome temptations if they are good! This is simply because temptations are not just good in themselves, but in how they exercise our spiritual lives as we go through them. And in going through them, the goal is to succeed so we can move on into higher levels of development in grace. When we face and gracefully overcome temptations, they lift us off onto different levels of our growth and walk with God. Through them we develop confidence and trust in God that we would not have otherwise.

Here are some ways to overcome temptations:

❖ Resist it
❖ Flee from it
❖ Destroy the source.

RESISTING TEMPTATION

Temptations as we have said is an opportunity for choice making, either for good or otherwise. However, as tests they are supposed to be opportunities for us to choose wisely and glorify God in the process. Ever since Adam and Eve took upon themselves the responsibility for their own choices; all mankind have had to continue making choices with each having its own consequences.

In some cases a person makes a choice, but the consequences are communal in nature. The consequences affect a whole lot more people than just the individuals who made the choice. This is what happened when Adam and Eve made their wrong choices. They subjected the whole humanity to the consequence of their failure.

But temptation is part of life systems that should not be dreaded or even avoided. There is a positive side to it. You can never develop spiritually by avoiding temptations, but by facing them in the power of God's Spirit. Only ignorant people claim they cannot be tempted. Besides, if one cannot be tempted then they will not amount to anything in God's purpose. It would also mean that their hearts are empty of any desires or dreams, which are the avenues for temptations.

Temptation as we observed earlier is basically the desire to indulge self, serve self, or seek self-glory or vainglory. Normally it plays on our desires deep within calling up on us to compromise and rationalize our convictions of the known will of God. But we are to resist such attempts by applying the principles of God's word silently or even loudly, if conditions allow. Such resistance must come from our deep and abiding relationship with God that we have developed over time.

That is where the fact of saturating oneself with God's word and presence, comes in. If we are not submitted to His will; our wills will not be subject to the restraints of His precepts and principles. In other words, neglecting close and deep personal relationship with God on a daily basis is to forfeit the very guidance and strength necessary to overcome temptations at the required moment.

Close fellowship with God apart from strengthening and giving insight, will also protect you from vulnerability to some obvious situations. We all face different situations that test our integrity daily, but godly inspiration is one of the keys to getting through such things. Overcoming temptation then begins with our faith in the realities of God's promises to us, and our reliance upon Him at all times. Applying the principles of His word, we can then stand against any temptations regardless of what those may involve.

At first it may seem like nothing is happening. It is just like looking at the sky at night; at first you do not seem to see anything, but then here and there a few stars appear. And the longer you look the more you see. That is how temptations are; at first you do not seem to be able to resist even the smallest ones. But the more you exercise yourself in faith resisting them, the more you develop in your inner being. This inner development should eventually move you from relying on *self* (senses) to relying on God and His provisions of grace. I think God makes it so, so that we do not become overconfident trying to lean on our past experiences.

Resisting temptation, therefore, is to deliberately choose the known Will of God. However, that is not always easy or popular in some cases. Sometimes even your own friends can misunderstand and ridicule you for doing that. Some of them may even consider you foolish or even old fashioned when you hold to personal integrity and refuse to indulge in some of their pastimes.

However, it is the best option standing firm in your convictions of God's word. It is putting *self* under submission to God and not giving in to any of its many desires for indulgences. It is standing up for God, enduring temptation without yielding. It is worth it, because in the end it is what will keep you going on consistently. Every temptation we overcome leads to our further development in God. Indeed, it is the choosing of good over evil what develops true virtue and godly character in us. Thus, your Christian perseverance in temptations is your way to victory.

Jesus is our example in this regard. He had unswerving relationship with the Father that helped Him resist the devil to the face. He displayed both perseverance and consistency. The devil had presumed that Jesus would bow down and worship him! But that in itself was repugnant to Jesus. He could not stand seeing someone not only playing God, but also demanding the worship and service that goes with it!

Consequently, He told the devil straight to the face to get out of His presence. Jesus did that in a very strongly worded statement, something like: "Enough is enough Satan get out of my face I do not have time for any more of your nonsense. How dare you ask me to worship you; don't you remember it is written *Thou shalt worship the Lord thy God, and him only shalt thou serve?* " Straightway Satan left Him.

Jesus had no room for the devil's type of dialogue anymore; the devil had taken his temptations unnecessarily far. But Jesus withstood him to the face and sent him packing. That is what it means to resist steadfast in the faith. We should all aspire and get to that point of steadfastness to face up to whatever situations and tell them "enough is enough we are not taking any more of you." That is how to get victory over some temptations; refusing them by the authority of God's word. The devil has no alternative when we resist him, but to flee.

As long as Jesus tried to be diplomatic with him, answering him in a gentleman's way; Satan always kept coming back with something else to tempt Him about. Being diplomatic with Satan is an exercise in futility, because trying to reason with him never makes any sense to him. He is so unreasonable. That is when Jesus ordered him to get lost from His face. From then on the devil never again tried any of his tricks on Him. That was the end of that whole episode of temptations. We can do the same, but only when we clearly understand the Father's Will, and are truly committed to Him.

FLEEING TEMPTATION

To balance our act in overcoming temptations, we may sometimes require going beyond just resisting. There are special situations, which call for special ways of response. In other words, overcoming temptations is not always in resisting alone. There is also the option of fleeing some particular situations.

Paul advices his readers in 2 Timothy 2:22 to flee youthful lusts and ungodly affections. He is not instructing them to resist youthful lusts (substance addictions, fornication and other sexual sins). If he did that he would be giving a wrong prescription that would be detrimental to his audiences' faith. People who try standing their ground in the face of sexual temptations, or substance intoxications almost always fail. In such matters sometimes you just have to take yourself out of the equation. Paul's command is to flee – run away as from terror, not to stand steadfast in the faith.

I like how Joseph did it in Potiphar's house. When his master's wife caught him by his cloak and demanded he sleeps with her; what did he do? Did he stand there to share his faith with her? Of course not. The only way to defeat the seduction queen then was what he did; bolt out. He fled the scene for his glorious faith. It was not an act of cowardice; he was simply applying godly wisdom. The best way to defeat some temptations is to flee from them like Joseph did in Genesis 39.

In fact, Paul himself fled *Iconium* in Acts 14:5-6. He did not just stand there in the face of his particular situation, resisting the revolt facing them believing he would stop it by "faith"! That would have ended in great loss of lives and ridicule to the gospel he was preaching. The only way he could overcome that situation was to flee.

Fleeing a situation (temptation) is not a denial of the power (anointing, presence) of God resident in us. But it is recognizing the weakness and vulnerability of the flesh, which is still much part of us. Fleeing situations as may be necessary is applying God's wisdom to overcome evil with good. By fleeing situations, we deny them any chances of finding expressions in and through us. The humbling wisdom is that sometimes it is far much better to run from situations, than to confront them. May God grant us the wisdom to know the difference!

DESTROY THE TEMPTATION INSTRUMENT

Some temptation situations are replayed or come to our lives as a result of being in possession of the execution instruments. The instruments used or employed in them are still with us. If we are to overcome such then we must get rid of certain things in our lives. These are things that remind us of our past involvements in or with those situations, thereby drawing us back into such sins.

They could be love letters, photos, books, albums, Ouija boards and so forth! We need to get rid of them and make no provisions for their luring us back into the sin situations. Even former friends, lovers, associates in sinful lifestyles and so forth; unless they are ready to fully embrace our Lord Jesus Christ, we should not entertain them deeply any longer. We must cut ourselves loose from every association that will remind us of or pull us back into sin.

AN EXAMPLE FROM THE BOOK OF ACTS

"And many that believed came and confessed, and shewed their deeds. Many of them also which used curious arts brought their books together and burned them before all men..." **Acts 19: 18-19.**

After these brethren believed in the Lord Jesus Christ, they destroyed their instruments of practice so as to defeat temptations and desire to go back into their old practices. The only way to overcome in such special and particular situations like this one is to burn the bridges behind you. Without the bridge you have got no way of retreating back into those pet situations. The simplest wisdom here is to distance yourself (take a break) from that which caused or causes you to sin. This may mean switching of the computer or TV or even changing of residences (states or cities) for some folks.

We see an example of this in the book of Luke 24 concerning the two disciples of Jesus who took a break from Jerusalem to go to Emmaus. They wanted to distance themselves from Jerusalem and the atmosphere of gloom and doom that then hanged over it. It is where their cherished dreams of acquiring their own kingdom exploded in their faces, and they felt they had been defeated when their Lord was killed.

In fact, there was no argument about it; Jerusalem according to them was not a place to be. They did not want anything more to do with it. They could not withstand the memory of the confusion that hanged over it. Based on the things that had just transpired there a few days gone by, everything was still very fresh in their minds. They could vividly remember the agonizing suffering that Jesus underwent toward His crucifixion. Anyone could be haunted especially if they had had an attachment to Him. Hence, they were cutting ties with it.

Victory for some situations in your life will only come as you opt to severe relations with your past. If you cannot take out what trips you; take yourself out of its sphere. In the gospels Jesus put it that if your right hand (or any other part, or thing) causes you to sin; take it away so it does not exist for the execution of that sin any more. In such cases, deliverance (victory) can only be attained by separation. There can be no deliverance without separation; if you want God's deliverance, you must be ready to separate from those old ties. But folks get defeated here because they want (desire) deliverance as well as to remain with those very things or situations. Clearly, it is dangerous for spiritual progress to ignore or hide the things we are supposed to destroy.

So far, we have observed that different situations call for different approaches. Thus, it is important to note that not every temptation is overcome the same way. Depending on their natures, some situations can be fled from while others you destroy the attraction object. The wisdom to know how to face the various situations we learn from our daily walk with God. This is important because applying a principle to a situation it does not correspond to will mean failure in that area. That means resisting temptation when you should be fleeing is unwise and will mean failure on your part. Or fleeing when you should be destroying the attraction object will not help much. That would be like running away from your own shadow. However, if you do not want the shadow; simply remove the light.

Similarly, if you want to do away with some temptation situations; you must remove the source. Destroy the execution instruments and no more attractions to those particular things. Then determine to walk with God faithfully, and He will bring you into a place in Him where you will commonly know your responses.

CHAPTER SIX

PURPOSE OF TEMPTATIONS

Apart from presenting us with an opportunity for choice making, which we should do in obedience to God; temptations also serve as means of testing (examining) us. They reveal what is of *man* and strengthen that which is of God in us. In other words, they blow open what is not solidly of God and thus reveal our humanness. They bring out or expose those areas in us where we are still spiritually weak; where we have not developed spiritually. They help us identify what negativity is still lurking inside us, and help us mark such so we can present them to God in prayers. Through them we also learn how to adjust spiritually by living according to God's Will. That means temptation is one aspect of the means for the accomplishment of God's purposes in and through us.

God lets them come to us because they are essential to our growth and character formation in the faith. They enable us to be established in trusting Him, and also help in strengthening that faith in Him. They are like exams that one has to take so as to graduate to the next grade in school. If you fail the exams, it gives you an opportunity to keep learning within that grade level until you acquire the necessary skills and understanding. That is to say, they are life hurdle in which we learn and grow in grace by depending on God.

This is one of the many reasons I say there is learning in failure. Someone put it that if you failed yesterday you can learn to live creatively today from that failure. If you spoke in anger without self-control, you should not repeat the folly today. If you keep lusting and having inordinate sexual thoughts, then you need to realize your problem the soonest. It is not others who cause you to lust or lie. Those are traits inside you and temptations come to help you see and break their connections. That is important so you do not keep doing the same incongruous things over and over.

That is where the Israelites were; stuck going round and round in the wilderness having failed to recognize and break the circle. They kept failing and never learning from their mistakes and they eventually ended up living in failure and their carcasses fell in the wilderness.

Though yielding to temptation is not the best option, sometimes there is much we can learn from failure than otherwise. We learn of our weaknesses, of God's unfailing faithfulness and the availability of His tender mercies to us in our times of need.

Thus, failing temptation is useful in the respect that it exposes those areas in us that we need not fool ourselves about. For example some people say, *"I did not mean to be mean or to get angry ... but you are the one who caused me to"* or words to such effects! The truth is, they got angry or acted mean because temper or meanness is still much alive in them. It is good they got angry or mean so it can be clearly displayed and help them discover the ugly face of temper or meanness still in them. It might be true someone did something, which infuriated them. Yet, those people's actions are not the basis for their meanness or anger! They got angry or acted mean because anger or meanness is still lurking in them somewhere.

Jesus taught that the things which defile a person, come from their inside.

> *And he said, That which cometh out of the man, that defileth the man. For from within, out of the heart of men, proceed evil thoughts, adulteries, fornications, murders, Thefts, covetousness, wickedness, deceit, lasciviousness, an evil eye, blasphemy, pride, foolishness: All these evil things come from within, and defile the man.* **Mark 7:20-23**

When you lust, steal, lie and so forth; you are only displaying what is in your heart. It is what is called the *evil* within us, which attracts the *devil* without. This gives meaning to Jesus' words; "The prince of this world comes but he has nothing in me". There was no evil within Him to attract the devil without. Even the scriptures testify that He was tempted in all ways as we are but He was without sin. When He was squeezed out of measure, to the last point of death, He pronounced forgiveness on those crucifying Him. Forgiveness is what came out of Him.

Nevertheless, failing temptation and learning from it is what I call **successful failure!** If we are wise we can learn inestimable things of importance from our mistakes. In fact, people can learn more from failure than from victory! No wonder, James advices Christians to count it all joy when they are tempted. Temptation in its every setting is a unique experience for learning.

> *"My brethren, count it all joy when ye fall into divers temptations"* **James1:2**.

James calls on us not to fear, tremble or run away from temptations but to count it **all** joy. He is not saying it is joyful being tempted. No, as a matter of fact, some temptation situations are rather very painful or even terrible experiences. Yet we hear James telling us to count it all joy. He is charging us to take the attitude of joyfulness in the midst of temptations. Why? Because the trying of our faith, works in us and helps us develop towards spiritual maturity.

In other words, temptations especially those we overcome help us develop in our inner lives. No one becomes a strong Christian simply by listening to sermons or attending church or Christian conferences, or even just by reading books. We have to undergo somethings so that we can be pressed accordingly, and in the process we grow spiritual muscles and strength. It is one of the means by which we grow up spiritually, going through and overcoming temptations. If we are never tested it is questionable, if we would develop and be stronger than otherwise.

Peter informs us that to be tempted is simply to be tested and refined; being fine-tuned in our spiritual life.

> *"These trials are only to test your faith, to see whether or not it is strong and pure. It is being tested as fire tests gold and purifies it – and your faith is far more precious to God than just mere gold. So if your faith remains strong after being tried in the test tube of trials, it will bring you much praise and glory and honor on the day of His return"* **1 Peter 1:7** (Living Bible)

Therefore, temptation is a means to growth and advancement in God. You grow and graduate into the next level of involvement with Him only by being tried and tested in your current level. If you go through successfully without breaking (failing) midway, then promotion or graduation awaits you. Like has been stated, *faith tested is faith strengthened;* whereas, untested faith in never known to grow strong.

There is a common saying that experience is a good teacher, and if so then temptation is the exam necessary from that teacher. It is a great circumstance for all Christian desiring fuller development in God.

CHAPTER SEVEN

DELIVERANCE IN TEMPTATIONS

"The Lord knoweth how to deliver the godly out of temptation . . . **2 Peter 2:9**.

Let us now turn to a few thoughts on deliverance in temptations, because as the above scripture indicates the Lord does deliver His people. Deliverance in temptations mainly comes:

BY CRYING OUT TO GOD

God knows our coming in and our going out; He even knows when we are in trouble, but in a number of situations He does not act unilaterally toward us. He awaits our invitation before He can come into our situations. Accordingly, every situation we find ourselves in, gives us an opportunity for calling on Him. He has promised that He would answer and show us great things when we call. Thus, we have to accept and express out our need of Him and His intervention. Receiving answers to our questions and desires lies in our asking Him.

Jonah serves as a good example here. Despite his earlier failures and rebellion against God, he decided to invite God into his overwhelming situation. He did not presume that since he had missed it once, then it was all right for him to continue in rebellion against God. That is what some of us do. When we miss it once we then throw away any lingering restraints, and go headlong into sin as a lifestyle. But not

Jonah. When the shipmaster caught up with him a sleep in the lower compartments and brought him to the others for questioning, he acted differently.

> *Then said they unto him, Tell us, we pray thee, for whose cause this evil is upon us; What is thine occupation? and whence comest thou? what is thy country? and of what people art thou? And he said unto them, I am a Hebrew; and I fear the LORD, the God of heaven, which hath made the sea and the dry land.* **Jonah1:8-9**.

He could have lied to them about everything they asked him. In fact, since he had run away from God he would have considered himself backslidden and he would have forgotten the whole matter of following God. But he refused to lie so as to save himself. Caught in similar situations, some of us would rather cheat, lie or make up stories to save our necks without considering our Christian witness and testimony.

Yet, here we see Jonah with the conviction of God's word still lingering in his heart, deciding to live by that conviction in contrast to the convenience of the time. His truthfulness in answering them even landed him into further and deeper problems. They ended up throwing him overboard!

> *Then Jonah prayed unto the LORD his God out of the fish's belly, And said,* **I cried** *by reason of mine affliction unto the LORD, and he heard me; out of the belly of hell cried I, and thou heardest my voice.* **Jonah 2:1-2**

He cried out unto the Lord and the Lord responded by speaking to the fish to vomit him out. And it did so at the right place and the right time within God's agenda for him then. The Lord delivered him from his predicament when he cried out. Cry out to the Lord and deliverance will be sure and swift.

BY GOD'S SOVEREIGN ACTS

There are some situations so overwhelmingly beyond anything we can ever do, except to resign ourselves over to God's sovereignty. An example of this was Peter's deliverance as narrated in (Acts 12:1-19.). Peter personally did nothing to instigate his rescue, even though the church prayed for him. But he personally resigned himself to God's sovereign will. His story reads thus:

Now about that time Herod the king stretched forth his hands to vex certain of the church. And he killed James the brother of John with the sword. And because he saw it pleased the Jews, he proceeded further to take Peter also. (Then were the days of unleavened bread.) And when he had apprehended him, he put him in prison, and delivered him to four quaternions of soldiers to keep him; intending after Easter to bring him forth to the people.

Peter therefore was kept in prison: but prayer was made without ceasing of the church unto God for him. And when Herod would have brought him forth, the same night Peter was sleeping between two soldiers, bound with two chains: and the keepers before the door kept the prison.

And, behold, the angel of the Lord came upon him, and a light shined in the prison: and he smote Peter on the side, and raised him up, saying, Arise up quickly. And his chains fell off from his hands. And the angel said unto him, Gird thyself, and bind on thy sandals. And so he did. And he saith unto him, Cast thy garment about thee, and follow me. And he went out, and followed him; and wist not that it was true which was done by the angel; but thought he saw a vision.

When they were past the first and the second ward, they came unto the iron gate that leadeth unto the city; which opened to them of his own accord: and they went out, and passed on through one street; and forthwith the angel departed from him. And when Peter was come to himself, he said, Now I know of a surety, that the Lord hath sent his angel, and hath delivered me out of the hand of Herod, and from all the expectation of the people of the Jews.

And when he had considered the thing, he came to the house of Mary the mother of John, whose surname was Mark; where many were gathered together praying. And as Peter knocked at the door of the gate, a damsel came to hearken, named Rhoda. And when she knew Peter's voice, she opened not the gate for gladness, but ran in, and told how Peter stood before the gate. And they said unto her, Thou art mad. But she constantly affirmed that it was even so.

Then said they, It is his angel. But Peter continued knocking: and when they had opened the door, and saw him, they were astonished. But he, beckoning unto them with the hand to hold their peace, declared unto them how the Lord had brought him out of the prison. And he said, Go shew these things unto James, and to the brethren. And he departed, and went into another place.

Now as soon as it was day, there was no small stir among the soldiers, what was become of Peter. And when Herod had sought for him, and found him not, he examined the keepers, and commanded that they should be put to death. And he went down from Judaea to Caesarea, and there abode.

CHAPTER EIGHT

THE GENERAL MEANS OF DELIVERANCE IN TEMPTATIONS

The issue of God's deliverance by sovereign acts generally takes the following forms:

- Through Guidance
- By Supplying His grace
- By godly environment or influence

DELIVERANCE THROUGH GUIDANCE

When faced with temptations, whether dealing with a moral dilemma like we saw in the story of Mr. Rayah; we often find ourselves powerless to resist some of those things. This is because generally human nature tends toward the forbidden. This is the reason we must always look to and rely on the Lord for help. Yes, there is deliverance by the Lord in temptations, but it is not automatic to all people. Only those intimate with Him will understand and experience this. Those in tune with Him alone will enjoy this blessing.

The Scriptures call them the godly. They are those who are abiding in Christ, living consecrated lives and walking in submission and obedience to Him. They do not willfully allow themselves into situations prone to selfish expressions and purposefully expose themselves to temptations. By this they cut themselves off and deny the temptations opportunities of expression through them. Seemingly, their steps are guided and ordered of the Lord. We can then say they are delivered from such temptation situations by God, through **guidance**. He guides them away from or makes them bypass some situations that otherwise, they selfishly would have easily indulged in to their moral detriment. They are guided or led of the Lord:

> *"For as many as are **led** (guided) by the Spirit of God are the sons of God"* Romans 8:14.

Our victory depends on God's guidance and there is no guidance to His Will anywhere else, but in Him. And obedience is the key to the Lord's guidance, in which trust and patience are also called into play as a verse from my poem *Faith the best option* portrays:

> *In faith Obedience the first step*
> *Followed by Trust and patience*
> *Abraham's life a clear portrayal*
> *Obediently left his domicile*
> *For a destination he knew not*
> *But hoping for the promise*
> *Father of many nations become*
> *In hope fervently confirmed*
> *Faith is the best option*

This is why the Bible admonishes us to,

> *"Trust in the Lord with all thine heart and lean not unto thine own understanding"*. **Proverbs 3:5**.

In this case victory is guaranteed, but only to those who trust in God. Trusting God rekindles their confidence in Him and His ability to fulfill His promises to them. Like has been said, there is no promise God made, which He does not intend to fulfill or that He cannot fulfill. He is faithful and able to do according to His Word. Yet, leaning on our own understanding implies dependence on ourselves. It makes us overestimate our ability to deal with situations in our lives on our own. This results in our entangling ourselves in them to the point of defeat.

Sometimes this happens when we draw inspiration from our previous experiences for current situations without involving God. Beloved, we can never receive God's victory by relying on ourselves. The truth is that when we rely on ourselves we will always fail temptations. To rely on *self* is simply to neglect His guidance that we need the most. He alone has the wider knowledge as to what attracts us to sin more than we do. That is because He has insight into the nature of our constitutions and beings, beyond what we are able to discern ourselves.

Consequently, to partake of His deliverance, our constant fellowship with Him is the key. It will enable us avoid situations that generate and make us vulnerable to temptations in the first place.

DELIVERANCE BY SUPPLY OF HIS GRACE

The second way of deliverance by God in temptations is by supplying us with His grace to stand and withstand situations. Somehow, if we get into temptations God *brings back to our memories the truth of His word* so that we can apply its principles to those situations. It is our application of those word-principles what triggers the working of His grace *to deliver us in those temptations*. He does that by rendering the temptations subservient to the accomplishment of His purposes.

This form of deliverance is where you are delivered, yet left to undergo the same temptation! What does this mean? It means God's deliverance in this respect is not to remove you from the temptation or make you escape it. Since you would have gotten into it; He lets you go through it anyway, but provides you with the necessary grace to take you through it successfully. It is like you never underwent it. The provision of His grace neutralizes the force of temptations and amplifies the conviction of His word in you, making it a cake walk for you.

The clear example here is Jesus Himself. When He faced the temptations, we observe that God did not remove Him from them. He let Jesus go through them, but supplied Him with grace unlimited. And He will do the same to any of us. He will not get you out of the temptation per se, but His grace supply will make it easy for you.

It is up to us to apply His word principles in whatever situations we are faced with. That is what even Jesus did; applying the word-principle, and He withstood the onslaught of all the temptations He faced. He went through them with grace in abundance and strength from on high.

Ignorantly, some of us presume and even pray whenever temptations come that God should remove them from us; or remove us from them. But that is not how it works. The Bible says, He will provide a way of escape *in the temptation*. You are to *escape in the temptation*. Some folks wonder how you are delivered when you are left to go through the same temptation! You go through it in the abundance of grace and it does not bother you much.

The apostle Paul in 1 Corinthians 10:13c seems to make this clear. The verse reads, especially from the King James Version:

"There hath no temptation taken you but such as is common to man: but God is faithful who will not suffer you to be tempted above that ye are able; but will with the temptation also make a way to escape, that ye may be able to bear it".

Some of us on reading this tend to understand that God will create a way *for us to* escape from the temptation so that we can be free from the same. But that is not it; it is not an escape from the experience of temptation or bad situations. Such an understanding is only looking for an exit out of the temptation, and has been called an escapists' mentality. It is the prevalent approach to temptations by many people who only seek deliverance or escape, rather than surrender to God's developmental agenda in such situations. God may be using some of such situations to develop and fulfill us.

The Apostle Paul himself might have been at such a point in his life when he prayed to God to remove his thorn in the flesh - the messenger of Satan. This was something he desired to be rid of, or even to escape. He thought he would have been a better person, able to work for God much better without it. Yet, God in His wisdom did not remove it; His answer to Paul's prayers implied he was better off with the thorn on his flesh and God's grace than without it!

"He said unto me, My grace is sufficient for thee, for my strength is made perfect in weakness" **2 Co 12:9**.

He asked for its removal, presumably, so he could freely do **greater** things for God. Yet God left it on him so that a **better** person he might become. That is God's unfathomable wisdom working very contrary to human reasons and understanding. He was not so much after greater works from Paul, but that a better person he was to become. He had a unique purpose for the thorn in the flesh in Paul's life. Hence, instead of removing it or providing a way for Paul to escape it; He supplied him with abundant grace to enable him bear it.

That is how it is even with us; most of us don't like temptations, and hence we always desire a way to escape from them. We even pray to God to get us out of them as quick as possible. But in most cases He does not, He leaves us in them so that we may develop and grow in grace. Based on His wisdom, He uses such situations to fulfill His purposes in us. What kind of a God would He be if He were to open a way for us to escape the very means He should use for the purpose of strengthening and developing us? If He did that He would be defeating His own purpose for us. Yet, He loves us so much to leave us in our infantile states. He will not suffer any of us to escape the very means of development in our Christian lives.

It is known that "full growth" or "full development" is His design in nature. And there is no difference even in grace. Why? Because anything less than full development or growth is sub-normal in His purpose and design. That is why He allows temptations into our lives, as some of the means to our spiritual developments. Nevertheless, He never allows greater temptations than we can handle.

"But God is faithful who will not suffer you to be tempted above that ye are able". **1 Corinthian 10:13b.**

From the Amplified Bible it reads;

"But God is faithful [to His word and to His compassionate nature] and He [can be trusted] not to let you be tempted and tried and assayed beyond your ability and strength of resistance and power to endure"

Let me paraphrase it:

"God in His faithfulness will definitely let you go through temptations yet, not anything beyond your ability to bear."

God measures out everything and knows what you can bear. That is why He expects you to stand your ground in the face of any of your temptations. Every temptation coming your way is within your ability to overcome, since anything beyond your ability to deal with He will not allow your way. He does that so His faithfulness to you remains undimmed in every situation and case. He has given each one of us a measure of faith through His grace, by which we are to bear up or go through such temptations successfully.

And the measure of that faith He divinely provides, having taken into full account all about you: your make-up frame, ethno-background, temperament and so forth. He tailors it specifically to enable you withstand and defeat the onslaughts from whichever quarters. Then having done that, you are to stand your ground with your loin girded with the belt of His truth.

Remember that apart from the resources He provides for you, He also has you in mind always. He does not abandon you even in the temptations. He is keenly watching over every situation with a view to supplying you with the necessary graces for them. It is that grace what will enable you go through such situations graciously and victoriously.

*"And God is able to make all **grace** abound toward you . . ."*
2 Corinthians 9:8a.

This is a wonderful an assurance that God makes **all** grace abound to you: the grace to stand, withstand and having done all; to stand. Therefore, do not listen to yourself; considering your strengths or weaknesses. That will only result into your defeat.

> ". . . *but will with the temptation also make* ***a way to*** ***escape***, *that ye may be able to bear it.*" 1 Corinthians 10:13c

Note that the verse does not say God provides a way *of* escape from, but a way *to* escape so that you may be able to bear it. If you were to escape it, why would He talk of you bearing it or being made able to bear it? This means, it is not talking about a way out of it, but into it! And that way is allowed with full provisions of His grace to take you over the temptation.

From other Bible versions that same part *c* reads:

> *"But with the temptation He will [always] also provide the way out – the means of escape to a landing place –* ***that you*** ***may be capable and strong and powerful, patiently to*** ***bear up under it"****. (Amplified Version).*

> *There hath no temptation taken you but such as man can bear: but God is faithful, who will not suffer you to be tempted above that ye are able;* ***but will with the*** ***temptation make also the way of escape, that ye may*** ***be able to endure it****. (American Standard Version).*

> *You have been put to no test but such as is common to man: and God is true, who will not let any test come on you which you are not able to undergo;* ***but he will make with the*** ***test a way out of it, so that you may be able to go*** ***through it****. (Bible in Basic English)*

*No temptation has taken you but such as is according to man's nature; and God is faithful, who will not suffer you to be tempted above what ye are able to bear, **but will with the temptation make the issue also, so that ye should be able to bear It**. (Darby Bible)*

*No temptation has overtaken you that is unusual for human beings. But God is faithful, and he will not allow you to be tempted beyond your strength. Instead, **along with the temptation he will also provide a way out, so that you may be able to endure it**. (International Standard Version)*

*No temptation has you in its power but such as is common to human nature; and God is faithful and will not allow you to be tempted beyond your strength. **But, when the temptation comes, He will also provide the way of escape; so that you may be able to bear it**. (Weymouth New Testament)*

All these versions state that you are provided with a way to escape so that you may be able to endure, withstand or bear and go through it. Thus, the way to escape in this regard is not an exit from the temptation, but provisions of grace to enable you withstand, or bear it successfully. That is His way by which you can be an overcomer in this respect. For your information, you will be much stronger after going through temptations successfully than if you never did. And like has been said, **an overcomer is someone who has *come over* some obstacle or thing without going around or under it.**

Hence, to overcome temptation you must go through it not around it, or run away from it. Temptation is the ground on which your victory is brewed or cast. Indeed, it is common knowledge that almost all Christians would like to be overcomers. But some want to do so without coming over anything; they think it is just a title. How ironical!

Nonetheless, God has promised us help in temptations and that help in some cases is in the form of His grace. That grace then translates into the required necessary strength and provisions, which He gives in such times of need.

DELIVERANCE THROUGH GODLY INFLUENCE

Another way of deliverance in temptations by the Lord is through the means of bringing, or surrounding us with **a godly influence**. Some temptations only come to us when we are alone or isolated (away) from those of the household of faith. This I believe is even Paul's reason for directing his readers in 2 Timothy 2:22, to follow righteousness, faith, charity, peace *with them that call on the Lord out of a pure heart*. The first part of his caution is to flee also youthful lust 2 Timothy 2:22. Then he directs them where to flee; to those of the same household of faith. By this, Paul was revealing what great treasures brethren are in the faith.

By running to them they become a means of deliverance from some forms of temptations through the influence of their presence, and the virtue of God's presence in their lives. Paul describes them as those who call upon the Lord out of a pure heart; purified through the working of His grace. God lets them into our lives for a reason, which we may not know straightaway. But His word implies that He sometimes works His good pleasures in our lives through these other believers.

As such, we need to recognize and respect other believers: their diversity, backgrounds, gifting and dignities. We must learn not to take them for granted. Always value your connections with them as God's significant and unique provisions for you in the journey of faith. He intends to use them to positively impact you.

How much more then should we be sensible in collaborating with and relying on each other, as we build trust in common pursuit of glorifying God. This is so because we are all divinely privileged people in whose lives God's mercy, and grace are at work. He does this for the purposes of enabling us to extend His influence in us as a provision for others in certain situations.

Somehow, even Elijah the Prophet got off a little when he got into murmuring and grumbling to God, presuming he was the only remaining true prophet of Jehovah in Israel then. But God corrected him, and His misconceptions cleared off. Thereafter, he called the people (the Israelites) to himself; to join him.

> *"And Elijah said unto all the people, come near unto me. And all the people came near unto him. And he repaired the altar of the Lord that was broken down."* **1 Kings 18:30**

He did not stand aloof continuing to presume he was the only righteous person in Israel. God did not want him to continue being indifferent to the people's conditions like he was not one of them. He had been called for the purpose of bringing those very people out of idolatry and Baal worship. God required him to mingle and co-exist with that rebellious backslidden and unbelieving generation of Israelites. He was not to wear some superiority (righteous) face and stand away from the rest of his brethren with a holier-than-thou attitude. As he accepted the prompting to join with the people again, God inspired (spoke to) him and he realized that the Lord's altar was in state of disrepair. He then took steps and carried out the necessary repairs. It is noteworthy that before he could offer any effective prayers or services to God, there had to be a reunion with the people first. Brethren are a resource unimaginable in God's purpose.

Jesus spoke about this in the New Testament when He said,

> *Therefore if thou bring thy gift to the altar, and there rememberest that thy brother hath aught against thee; Leave there thy gift before the altar, and go thy way; first be reconciled to thy brother, and then come and offer thy gift.* **Matthew 5:23-4**

Love, understanding and tolerance towards the brethren are major building blocks for lasting Christian relationships. And such relationships are a buffer or a means of deliverance in temptations. Thus, we ought to develop and nurture frank relationships with others based on God's love for all of us. Moreover, if we walk in love as He is love then we will have proper relationships one with another.

Rightly so, James charges us to:

> *"Speak not evil one of another brethren, he that speaketh evil of his brother speaketh evil of the law..."* **James 4:11** (KJV)

Evil speaking is a subtle practice common even among believers, in which they foul mouth others; speaking evil of and criticizing them behind their backs. But in God's calling the Apostle Peter portrays that we are all living stones being built together into God's glorious and wonderful design. That is a great mystery and privilege for all of us to be intimately involved with. There is room for everyone willing to be found in Him, and as such there is no need of tearing others down with malicious words.

Sometimes folks excuse their foul mouthing others by claiming they are just saying the truth. But it has also been pointed out that truth must be spoken in love. Since, gossip and criticism of others are usually never done in love; they are unacceptable practices even if there is some truth in the claims. Paul says,

Finally, brethren, whatsoever things are true, whatsoever things are honest, whatsoever things are just, whatsoever things are pure, whatsoever things are lovely, whatsoever things are of good report; if there be any virtue, and if there be any praise, think on these things. **Philippians 4:8**

The stories may be true, but are they of good report? Or are they honest things that can be mentioned about one to whom Christ died? Even if there is truth in any given matter; we should not engage in unloving acts of repeating such. We have not been called into the faith to destroy others, and thereby the body of Christ. But rather we have been called to love one another fervently. Hence, our words must be guided by love not just by truth alone. Let us be given to the edification of the brethren and building them up as much as it is in our power.

God says it is blessed when brethren dwell together in unity and upon such, He commands His blessings even life eternal. How important it is then to live in harmony with the brethren, maturing into (what Paul calls perfecting) holiness, without which no one will see God! Brethren are a mighty tool in God's hands towards influencing or provoking us to godly living and good works. Someone wisely put it that then we are all directly related to each other in the Lord. As such we are all members of His one Body influencing how our brethren live and function.

"So let us seize and hold fast and retain without wavering the hope we cherish and confess, and our acknowledgement of it, for He who promised us is reliable (sure) and faithful to His word". **Hebrews 10:23** (Amplified Version.)

Let each one of us, therefore, take our rightful place in Him informed by the fact that we are the Father's provision to others. Indeed, we are our brothers' keepers; a godly atmosphere and means of deliverance in their certain situations.

To recap, the Lord delivers in temptations:

❖ Through Guidance
❖ By Supplying His grace
❖ By a godly influence

CHAPTER NINE

SUMMARY OF FACTS ABOUT TEMPTATIONS

- *Temptation is universal*; found everywhere, especially where people are. And no one can claim exception.
- *Temptation* finds its force in and is governed by certain things in life; codes; ethical or moral, but not limited to morality and yielding to sin.
- *Temptation is always present tense.*
- *Temptation is common;* a phenomenon from our daily experiences.
- *Temptation comes to everyone*: in their own way
- *Temptation will always be, in this life.* As long as we are in the housing of our bodies.
- *Temptation questions and casts shadow on God's character* pitting our wills against His; promising us happiness, significance and security acquired our own way.
- *Temptations are deceptive appearances.* They are a spiritual mirage.
- *Temptations always challenge our resolve and belief (knowledge) about our stand for God.*
- *Temptation presents us with an opportunity for choice making.* However, not every act of choosing is a form of temptation!
- *Temptations are usually recurring phenomena.* That is, temptations unlike opportunities will always give you a second chance.
- *Temptation is not by any means, a proof of lack of spirituality,* nor a sign of weakness but rather it is a sign of

your commitment to walking with God, hence the negative factors that arise to derail you.

- *Temptations are among the means of growth in grace when faced and gracefully overcome.*
- *Temptation is progressive* from the element of **distrusting** God and then lusting or having **inordinate desires** and eventually **disobeying** Him by yielding to such desires

BASIC COMPARISONS BETWEEN JESUS AND ADAM'S TEMPTATIONS

Temptation One: About things physical – body and its satisfaction; catering to the flesh.
- Adam – selfishly chose to *eat* from the tree of knowledge of good and evil
- Jesus – tempted to turn stones into bread with a view to *eating* but refused

Temptation Two: Was on the religious sphere or religious temptation.
- Adam was asked – Did *God* really say . . . ?
- Jesus – was told about *angels* ready to hold Him if He chose to jump from the *temple* pinnacle

The terms **God, angels and temple** as used in the conversation with the two human fountainheads were emblems of religion. Hence, this was a religious temptation.

Temptation Three: Was about pride of life (power and glory)
- To Adam – you will become God
- To Jesus – promised power and glory of ruling all kingdoms

Generally, temptations are in these three major categories:
- With physical things (materialism) – about our body and its satisfaction and things that please the eyes

- With Religious and intellectual things reasoned in the mind
- With ornate abstract things involving power and glory (exaltation, pride, anger and so forth) to feed the ego.

LAST WORD

Finally, with the foregone clarifications and insights on temptations; let us then press on with God, embracing whatever tests or temptations He allows our way. Let us rest assured that God will never leave us, nor forsake us. Besides all temptations He allows are measured to our persona, intended to make us the people of His full intentions. It is in such situations that we can **score** highly in His purposes. That is, we can:

S - Selflessly undertake responsible and faithful stewardship in fulfilling His call in us, functioning morally and ethically, in all our undertakings.

C - Collaborate with and rely on each member of His body as part of God's family, building trust and striving for the same goal of glorifying our Father.

O – Organize properly and carefully to allow orderliness, with each one in his or her place, from whom the whole body, joined and knit together by what every (member) joint supplies, according to the effective working by which every part does its share, causes growth of the body for the edifying of itself in love.

R – Recognize and respect the diverse backgrounds, gifting and dignity of the wider members of the fellowship of His body. We must accept to function together with understanding and tolerance not demanding uniformity.

E – Encourage efficiency in ministry functions, carrying out regular (peer) evaluations, and allowing for new ideas as

Moses did in accepting **the Jethro principle** to prevent being rigid in the moves of God.

I trust that the simple message of this book has given you an appropriate understanding of and insight into temptations. Now walk faithfully with God without fearing any form of temptations. And I pray that His grace will abound unto you in all things as you progress and mature in Him, always remembering that

"...**when** the **temptation comes,** He will also provide the way of escape; so that you may be able to bear it". 1 Corinthians 10:13c, (Weymouth New Testament).

Blessings to you. Thanks for your time. Please drop us a line and let us know how you have personally benefited from reading this book. Address your correspondences to the Address at the front of the book, or better still e-mail: **greatministries@yahoo.com**

www.ingramcontent.com/pod-product-compliance
Lightning Source LLC
Chambersburg PA
CBHW060818050426
42449CB00008B/1723